The Strands Entwined

The Strands Entwined

A · NEW · DIRECTION IN · AMERICAN · DRAMA

SAMUEL J. BERNSTEIN

NORTHEASTERN UNIVERSITY PRESS
BOSTON 1980

Editors, Robilee Smith & Kathy Talmadge
Book and Cover Design, Mary Owanesian

Library of Congress Cataloging in Publication Data
Bernstein, Samuel J   1937-
The Strands Entwined.
Bibliography: p.
Includes index.
1. American drama—20th century—History
and criticism. I. Title.
PS351.B4   812'.54'09   80-12740
ISBN 0-930350-07-3
Printed in the United States of America

I dedicate this book to my wife, Arlene;
to my parents, Frances and Leon Bernstein;
to my children, Karyn, Danny, and Joshua;
and to my sister, Edythe, and her family.
Their love, loyalty, and steadfast
encouragement have sustained me in this and
in all my endeavors.

Preface

A recurrent theme—actually the thesis—of a lecture delivered by Walter Kerr in November 1976, as guest speaker of the Boston College Humanities Series, was that our American drama is at a low ebb.[1] He suggested that not only are we suffering from a dearth of fine playwrights, but the prospect of the emergence of a significant American drama does not currently exist. Like Stanley Kauffmann and others, Kerr has found merit in individual plays, but he sees these sporadic expressions as only moderately exciting in themselves and hardly indicative of a dramatic renaissance.

While I have the deepest respect for Mr. Kerr as a reviewer, theatre historian, and genre theorist, I believe that he and numerous colleagues are in error in this judgment and prophecy; I see a new wave of American playwrights of high calibre, playwrights who have already begun to demonstrate their talents. Additionally, I believe that some established playwrights are also producing new works of merit. Therefore, dramatic offerings of the 1970s bode well for our theatre's future; in fact, they constitute early evidence that we have entered upon a new era of American playwriting, an era of works that compare favorably with those produced between the late forties and early sixties by Miller, Williams, Inge, and Albee. In fact, I believe these current works will do justice to the American dramatic heritage left us by Eugene O'Neill.

An overview of the new playwrights and novel techniques, even though many of them are admittedly purely sensational and hardly interesting, reveals a rather subtle similarity of impulse. In a few gifted writers this impulse, the mingling of two important strains in our national dramaturgy, has resulted in a true and new harmony. These two strains are the realistic–naturalistic, the traditionally dominant orientation of American drama, and the European Absurdist, which has developed over the last fifty years, most predominantly through the works of Samuel Beckett, Eugene Ionesco, Jean Genet, and Harold Pinter.

The examination of this impulse, this recent congenial blending of the realistic–naturalistic and the European Absurdist strains, is the subject of this study, which presents a thesis running counter to that of Mr. Kerr. Once elucidated in the works of five current playwrights, then extrapolated and discussed theoretically, it should serve, I believe, as the basis for a new understanding and a more optimistic assessment of current American drama.

In trying to write a book about recent American drama I must admit, at the outset, that I have had to make an arbitrary time delimitation. I am concentrating upon plays professionally produced in the early 1970s. It is difficult to judge whether the so-called "winding down" and conclusion of the Vietnam war in the early 1970s brought about a fundamental change in both America and its drama; surely, even the late 1960s permitted an overview of the Southeast Asian situation that an earlier period did not permit. Surely, American drama of the 1970s has in some measure reflected the meaning of return from war. Yet no confident statement can be made relating the drama of the 1970s directly to that experience, and many of the most distinguished plays of the 1970s seem utterly unconcerned with the war or its effect on American society.

Consequently, this book begins with few assumptions and no rigid boundaries imposed by the culture at large. I have simply chosen five plays that I believe to be distinguished examples of current American drama. Two of these plays were actually written in the late 1960s by new playwrights. David Rabe's *Sticks and Bones* appeared in 1968, and Act I of John Guare's *The House of Blue Leaves* was performed as early as 1966, although he continued revising Act II until the end of the decade. Robert Anderson's *Double Solitaire* appeared in 1971; in 1975, both Ed Bullins' *The Taking of Miss Janie* and Edward Albee's *Seascape* appeared.

This study does not aim to be a comprehensive overview of all dramatic genres; it makes no attempt to assess the contribution of feminist drama, audience participation drama, the Theatre of Nudity, the Theatre of Cruelty, actor-created drama, choric collages, or monodrama, all of which are very interesting in themselves. Also, the study admittedly reflects personal tastes in its very choice of material. Despite the study's necessary boundaries, I believe that it presents a view of the current state of our drama and of our present American ethos as it is reflected in that drama.

For some time American drama has received rough treatment by many of our most intelligent and perceptive critics. In the fifties, Robert Brustein criticized the sensationalism and alleged sexual fixation of American dramatists.[2] Since then Brustein, with rare exception, has found American plays unsatisfying. Their deficiency in ideas, he has claimed, puts them at a disadvantage when compared with European works. Similarly, Mary McCarthy has complained that a lack of distinguished language mars our plays.[3] Perhaps the most damning criticism of all has been made by Alvin Kernan in his introduction to *Modern American Theater: A Collection of Critical Essays* (1967). There he suggests that American drama has been a failure compared with our novels and poetry, citing as exceptions only five plays comparable in quality to our highest achievements in the other genres. The five plays he considers exceptions are *The Skin of Our Teeth, Long Day's Journey into Night, Death of a Salesman, A Streetcar Named Desire,* and, added "somewhat more hesitantly," *The Zoo Story.*[4] If we need yet more testimony, Stanley Kauffmann, as critic for *The New Republic,* has continually pointed out the shortcomings of our playwrights, particularly those who have been greatly praised by his colleagues. He has found several major flaws, including sentimentality, trite language, and stale theatrical techniques.

To provide an adequate answer to each portion of these diverse negative judgments would take an entire book in itself. However, since a defense of the whole body of modern American drama is not within the scope of this study, let me simply assert that since the time of O'Neill, American drama may be favorably compared with that of any nation throughout the world. And since I believe the modern period to be one of the great periods in dramatic art—the others being the Greek, the Shakespearian, and the neoclassic French—this constitutes a rather considerable claim for the quality of the American plays.

While many critics and scholars confidently employ such criteria as the deficiency of ideas, lack of poetry, or even the derivative practices of many of our playwrights, I am not convinced that such measures can be meaningfully employed to evaluate our drama. To me, the ultimate question is: what is the theatrical experience—its rhythms, its symbolic connections, its capacity to make one feel keenly? I believe that the best American plays, and there are a significant number, put one in touch with the resources of one's own humanity, with the ethos of a nation, and with the dynamics of the human experience. If the relation of ideas to language and movement in a play in some way produces an intensified sensibility (Unamuno's "felt thought"[5]), then the play is valuable.

Since 1967, when Kernan made his highly negative assessment of American drama, there have been many new plays produced; some of them have been as distinguished as the works of Miller, Williams, Inge, and Albee—the giants of the late forties, fifties, and early sixties—and a few can be considered as even comparable with the works of O'Neill. Between the 1962 production of *Who's Afraid of Virginia Woolf?* and the late sixties, our drama was not particularly exciting, primarily because it seemed not particularly substantial or finished. In the middle sixties, American theatre generally failed to harmonize image and idea and to mirror with any depth the currents of our national or personal experience. From 1962 to 1969, only three serious American plays were awarded Pulitzer Prizes; these included Frank Gilroy's *The Subject Was Roses* (1965), Edward Albee's *A Delicate Balance* (1967), and Howard Sackler's *The Great White Hope* (1969). During the same period, the New York Drama Critics' Circle Award for Best Play went almost exclusively to foreign playwrights. In fact, only two truly distinguished American plays were produced during this time: *America Hurrah* by Jean Claude Van Itallie and *The Old Glory* by Robert Lowell. Although neither play won a major dramatic award, each is a masterpiece in its own way. *America Hurrah* employed fresh surrealistic images and extremely flexible theatrical techniques to explore the tawdriness, violence, plasticity, and numbness of our culture; and *The Old Glory* provided the most exquisite poetry to inform a dramatic work in our nation's history.

Such high praise for these two works might imply that we ought to begin our analysis at an earlier date. Not so, for although *America Hurrah* and *The Old Glory* are artistic works of a very high order, they are truly idiosyncratic expressions, tours de force (pure surrealism in one case; pure poetry in another) that are outside the mainstream of our drama and peripheral to what I discern to be the central impulse of the current scene. In essence, these works were simply the best expressions of the middle sixties, a period of trial and error that is best remembered for the groundbreaking experiments of such groups as The Living Theatre and Café La Mama. Although these groups lost their vitality in the seventies, we are reaping the benefits of their experimentalism, which has been significantly and profitably fused with other, more substantial cultural impulses. For this reason, more current drama and playwrights are truly worthy of serious attention.

Several of these recent writers and works epitomize a change in our drama that bodes well for our future; this new direction in American drama constitutes the principal focus of this book. My method is to provide a general overview of the modern American theatre (Chapter I), followed by individual considerations of five plays of the present period (Chapters II–VI), and a final consideration of the changes in American drama and culture, exemplified through these critical surveys and discussions (Chapter VII).

To afford some notion of the reception and reputation of each playwright, and to elucidate some of the foci of critical debate, the discussion of each play begins with a review of the major published criticism on it.

The reviews of the criticism are characterized by an essentially nonjudgmental inclusion of a broad range of critics. Some of these critics write for daily papers or weekly or monthly magazines whose critical standards are less distinguished than others and which are certainly less often reliable gauges of dramatic quality than the critical outlets of such a writer as Walter Kerr, a substantial scholar who has written numerous respected books and articles. Furthermore, the criticism herein cited includes both quick-reaction assessments of performances, geared exclusively to the popular readership, and longer, more carefully considered and acute reactions to the plays as works of art. My reason for this inclusive, essentially egalitarian attitude to the criticism is that the newness of the styles of the plays herein discussed has sometimes surprisingly (some might say *predictably*) produced flashes of true insight among less distinguished critics and error and superficiality of judgment by those who are usually more incisive. Furthermore, I simply have not found the ideas in the carefully constructed, sophisticated articles or essays sufficiently different from the ideas expressed more briefly in the popular press in attitude toward, or understanding or appraisal of, the works of my study. Again, these works are new, and I hope that from a serious scholarly/critical perspective this somewhat innovative approach to the criticism is justifiable and may prove helpful in this study.

The survey of criticism on each play leads to a discussion of that work, based on a close reading with intermittent commentary that emphasizes important strains or qualities. Each discussion section then concludes with a separately designated consideration of the relation of realism to Absurdism, the two major strains in each of the works.

The works I have selected to include in this study are: *Sticks and Bones* by David Rabe, which concerns the return home of a blinded Vietnam veteran and the friction that arises between himself and his conventionally middle-class family; *The House of Blue Leaves* by John Guare, which explores the chaotic life and frustrations of a zookeeper/would-be songwriter, as he searches feverishly and fruitlessly for fame and fortune; Ed Bullins' *The Taking of Miss Janie*, a long one-act play that concerns black/white relations in the 1960s; *Double Solitaire* by Robert Anderson, which exposes the lack of satisfaction and spirit in a middle-aged marriage; and, finally, Edward Albee's *Seascape*, which presents a more lengthy investigation of a middle-aged couple faced with a critical need for meaning—not simply in their marriage, but in life itself.

Notes

[1]Walter Kerr, "The Remaking of the American Theatre," lecture given at Boston College, Newton, Mass. (2 November 1976).

[2]Robert Brustein, "Why American Plays Are Not Literature," *Harper's*, 219 (October 1959), pp. 167–172. *See also:* Brustein, "The Theater of Middle Seriousness: A Report on the Broadway Season," *Harper's*, 218 (March 1959), pp. 56–63.

[3]Mary McCarthy, "The American Realist Playwrights," *On the Contrary* (New York: Farrar, Strauss & Cudahy, 1961), p. 295.

[4]Alvin Kernan, "Introduction," *Modern American Theater: A Collection of Critical Essays* (Englewood Cliffs, New Jersey: Prentice-Hall, 1967), p. 1.

[5]Miguel de Unamuno, "Don Quixote Today," *Tragic Sense of Life*, trans. J. E. Crawford Flitch (New York: Dover, 1954), p. 314.

Acknowledgments

This book is an outgrowth of years of study and teaching. In a very real sense, it is impossible to assess the contributions of students and colleagues to this project. Their contributions, nevertheless, have been great; my debt to them is considerable and, in many cases, of long standing. Fortunately, it is possible to mention some people who have had a clear and direct influence upon the book. Those to whom I am most indebted are Lita Wright, a former graduate student, who assisted me in the early stages of the research; William Frohlich, Director of the Northeastern University Press, and his entire staff; but most prominently Robilee Smith, who supervised the entire project; and Judith Brudnick, who made helpful observations on the text and who enabled me to communicate with the Press in a smooth and efficient manner. I cannot praise too highly the work of Kathy Talmadge, the copy editor, and of my wife, Arlene. Their suggestions on style and content were truly invaluable. I am also deeply grateful to Professors Leonard Berkman, Leonard Casper, and James Clay, whose comments on the manuscript enabled me to refine and clarify my presentation. I, of course, assume total responsibility for the style and content of the book.

Contents

Modern American Drama: An Overview

I

*T*o describe the parameters of American drama is at best an extremely difficult task; in any nation, artistic expression is always resistant to generalization, and American drama is particularly difficult to define because of its vast diversity. Nevertheless, to speak of American drama is, in large measure, to speak of Eugene O'Neill (1888–1953). He is our giant and our genius; he can be credited with lifting American theatrical and dramatic art from the stagey artificiality of the nineteenth- and early twentieth-century imitations of English and diluted European models to a drama of consequence and originality.

O'Neill wrote more than sixty plays during a period of over forty years. Although some of these plays he purposely destroyed, most of them are yet preserved. Not all of O'Neill's surviving plays and nonfiction writing are accessible; just before his death, O'Neill stipulated that no one be allowed to read certain material until twenty-five years had passed. His third wife, Carlotta Monterey O'Neill, then further restricted access to the material, the greater part of which is held in the archives of the Yale University Library.

O'Neill's stipulation has already been violated on a number of occasions, most prominently in the production of *Long Day's Journey into Night*, one of O'Neill's outstanding works and perhaps among that small group of modern American plays that will live and grow in stature through the decades. Also prematurely unearthed and successfully produced was *A Touch of the Poet*, part of O'Neill's projected cycle of eleven plays that were to trace the life of an Irish American family; *More Stately Mansions* also belongs to this cycle. Unfortunately, O'Neill's full cycle of plays remained unfinished at the time of his death.

This premature unearthing of O'Neill's protected plays was made possible by Carlotta Monterey O'Neill, who was deeply impressed by José Quintero's sensitive mounting of an earlier play, *The Iceman Cometh* (1956). Over the objection of Bennett Cerf of Random House, who was entrusted to preserve the plays unseen and unproduced until 1978, she gave permission to have the plays presented. These early productions enabled us to see more fully the contours, including several of the peaks, of O'Neill's writing career.

In essential matters of lifestyle and outlook, O'Neill differed radically from his father, the prominent actor James O'Neill. However, he learned much from his father. James had come to the United States from Ireland as an impoverished boy and rose to wealth and fame as the star of *The Count of Monte Cristo*. As James O'Neill's son, Eugene had a permanent entry into theatrical circles. He saw productions mounted from conception to conclusion. He listened as the leading actor practiced his lines, and he became particularly intrigued with the many stage devices and tricks that were employed to create a sense of illusion in the eyes and minds of the audiences. These early experiences in the theatre had a powerful effect on O'Neill's writing. Learning so intimately, as he did, of the unlimited resources of the theatre, O'Neill was able to become—to borrow the notion of Jean Cocteau—a poet of the theatre. For Dr. Alan Downer, former Princeton University theatrical and literary critic and historian, the phrase "poetry of the theatre" refers to an artist's ability to adapt and harmonize the theatre's innumerable resources for his particular imaginative ends.[1] O'Neill, as a "poet of the theatre," knew how to create total theatre; that is, he mastered the art of combining set, makeup, props, sound effects, lighting, and a host of other elements to create the necessary intensity of atmosphere for each individual play.

To see O'Neill's work in terms of this formulation is to encounter his experimentalism, one of the major characteristics of his playwriting, and the characteristic that leads most predominantly to his remarkable artistic diversity. In the 1960 issue of *Modern Drama*, a commemorative issue dedicated entirely to Eugene O'Neill and his writing, Arthur A. Nethercot makes the astounding statement that, by the year of O'Neill's death, critics were unable to assert that any single O'Neill play was "typical" of his canon.[2] Although, as Nethercot goes on to suggest, there is a discernible unifying pattern in O'Neill's work, scholars and critics remain struck by his spellbinding variety and richness of technique.

His technical virtuosity is evident in his earliest one-act plays published by his father, and it deepens in the slightly later one-act plays, more complex in effect and characterized by multi-scenic sequences. This virtuosity enabled him to create plays of two acts, four acts, and five acts. The five-act dramas, which were particularly influenced by his close reading of Shakespeare and the Greeks during a period of convalescence from tuberculosis in his mid-twenties, include such titanic dramas as *Mourning Becomes Electra* and *Strange Interlude*. In production, these plays last five to six hours, and are somehow able to sustain a lengthy intermission for a dinnertime meal.

To reflect upon the O'Neill canon is to bring to mind experiments in naturalism, such as *Beyond the Horizon*, which in 1920 won him his first of four Pulitzer Prizes; it also brings to mind examples of surrealism and expressionism, as in *The Hairy Ape* and *The Emperor Jones*. Moreover, it brings to mind such plays as *The Great God Brown*, in which realism and surrealism are powerfully, if not always gracefully, fused. A list of O'Neill's innovations and imaginative uses of traditional effects would be almost endless: the giant, insensitive puppets emerging from the church in *The Hairy Ape*; the extensive use of the choral chanting in *Lazarus Laughed*; the splitting of the personality into ego and alter ego in *Days Without End*; the magnificent dialect and geometric structure of *The Iceman Cometh*; and, of course, the unforgettable haunting tom-toms of *The Emperor Jones*, initially seventy-two pulse beats per minute and rising in tempo as the audience (as well as the anguished emperor) is brought to a feverish pitch until the play's compelling and inevitable conclusion.

Although O'Neill's achievement is unparalleled, the diversity of his writing is representative of American drama in general. America has been a seedbed of realism, surrealism, naturalism, expressionism, poetic drama, philosophical drama, the pantomimic theatre, the Theatre of Cruelty, the Theatre of Nudity, and a host of additional dramatic and theatrical postures described so well by Robert Brustein in his collection of essays entitled *The Third Theatre*[3] and by Stuart Little in *The Prophetic Theater*.[4]

While diversity is clearly one characteristic of our drama, the sharply divided critical reaction to Edward Albee's plays indicates another major characteristic, optimism. In *Edward Albee: Playwright in Protest*, Michael Rutenberg has aligned himself with those who consider Albee to be primarily a social critic.[5] However, Martin Esslin includes Albee in his study entitled *The Theatre of the Absurd*,[6] in which Albee is considered the only non-European Absurdist playwright. These apparently contradictory assessments of Albee's function arise from Albee's blend of the essentially logical and optimistic nature of social protest drama and the disjunct and pessimistic orientation of Absurdist drama, which belongs to the tragic mode. To deny the strain of social protest in Albee's drama would, of course, be ludicrous; only a social critic could have written *The Death of Bessie Smith*. On the other hand, the dissolution and demise of Jerry in *The Zoo Story* or the Lear-like stripping of supports from George and Martha in *Who's Afraid of Virginia Woolf?* are neither laughable nor entirely resolvable matters. Surely, George and Martha are cleansed and purified by the destruction of their pipe dreams, particularly their illusions about their nonexistent son; yet, as they finally stand, clinging to each other and culturally bare and frightened, they face darkness and the void. It is fair, therefore, to say that however one assesses the relative importance of Albee's elements of social criticism and tragedy, both elements exist and both function richly and meaningfully in relation to each other. However bleak, however Absurdist, however serious and hopeless the ultimate vision of an Albee play may be, all negativism and pessimism are surely diluted by a highly sanguine strain, which provides a strikingly different aura and atmosphere than we find in the European works included in the Esslin study.

Even in O'Neill's works, we may rightfully denote a similar condition. O'Neill has been termed a pessimist more frequently and consistently than any other American writer. Only one comedy, *Ah, Wilderness!*, appears in his known works, and as a comedy it is not without its wistfulness. In his chapter "The Tragic Fallacy" in *The Modern Temper*, Joseph Wood Krutch denied the possibility of tragedy in the modern world; paradoxically, he found in O'Neill's work true Greco-Elizabethan heroism, grandeur, and magnificence of character, which led him to consider O'Neill a tragedian. Because Krutch believed that the glorious expression of man's possibilities is an important element in tragedy, he denied that tragedy must ultimately be based in negativism and pessimism.[7]

In Krutch's assetion of O'Neill's life affirmation, in his exclusion of *The Iceman Cometh* from the acceptable tragic canon, we learn not so much about tragedy as about O'Neill and, ultimately, about American drama. Krutch was quite right in finding an affirmative element in O'Neill's work and quite wrong in calling him a tragedian, except perhaps in *The Iceman Cometh*, that very play from which he recoiled because of its nihilism and perverse negativism. To scrutinize carefully the source of Krutch's sensitive and comprehensive response to O'Neill is to discover that O'Neill's affirmative element is not a part of the tragic mode, as Krutch asserted; rather, it is completely alien to the tragic mode. This affirmative element, which in some measure runs through all of O'Neill's plays, is a religious strain, a strain that, by contrast to the tragic machinery and impulse, is assuredly latent; however, it ultimately arises with great dramatic power in each O'Neill play (excluding, perhaps, *The Iceman Cometh*) to transcend the tragic line of development at the climatic moment, thereby dominating the play's aesthetic. Therefore, O'Neill must be considered a tragico-religious writer, ultimately sanguine, ultimately hopeful.

The optimism in the works of O'Neill and Albee is also characteristic of the body of American drama. Surely, there are negative, pessimistic American works; but, in most instances, the thorough bleakness to be found in the Absurdist strain of the European writers is diluted in the American works by a positive, affirmative, high-spirited orientation. This hopefulness is a second major characteristic of American drama.

O'Neill once said that if he were to be properly appreciated, it would have to be as a poet. He was speaking literally; and in the employment of rhythmic speech, examples of which include the stichomythia of *Desire Under the Elms* and the chanting of *Lazarus Laughed*, we can see some merit in his claim. To be objective, however, it would not be accurate to describe O'Neill as a poet, as one would describe Shakespeare, Racine, or even Harold Pinter, if by poetry we refer to the imaginative exploration of the resources of language. Rather, O'Neill's language belongs, with some qualification, to the realistic–naturalistic mode of dialogue.

Mary McCarthy has sharply criticized this mode of dialogue—in works not only by O'Neill, but by Miller, Williams, and other American playwrights. She points out that the truly poetic, memorable lines in American drama are so few that they contrast sharply with the dialogue of plays in which poetic lines do not exist.[8] For example, in Tennessee Williams' *The Glass Menagerie*, who can forget Amanda's painful reflection upon the departure of her husband:

> I married a man who worked for the telephone company!—That gallantly smiling gentleman over there! (*points to the picture*) A telephone man who—fell in love with long-distance![9]

It would be difficult to imagine a richer, more economical expression of a multiplicity of interrelated details—the pain of separation and the linkage of job, American milieu, and condition of mind—as well as of the character of the handsome man with whom Amanda fell foolishly in love in her youth. In that same play, we might mention the incomparable jonquils monologue in which Amanda recreates her early infatuations, providing us with a perfect illustration of Archibald MacLeish's dictum in "Ars Poetica" that "A poem should not mean/But be."[10] But both of these poetic moments are linguistically atypical of the play and of the body of Williams' writing. The impression that Williams is a "poetic" writer is created by his sensitive treatment of helpless or suffering individuals. Moreover, his employment of music and similar dramatic resources to enrich his fables adds to this impression. But although occasional monologues are superb arias, poetic gems, and although independent lines are at times poetic, his dialogue cannot be generally described as "poetic." In numerous instances, he strives to be poetic, but he is rarely successful; for example, *Camino Real* is severely weakened by almost parodic passages. Williams is a great writer who employs human understanding, theatrical variety, and selective poetry to achieve his aims, but he is not "poetic."

O'Neill, too, is not "poetic," but to find poetry in O'Neill's works we need only to consider Nina's reflection in *Strange Interlude*: "Our lives are merely strange dark interludes in the electric display of God the Father,"[11] or Edmund's trenchant yet poignant comment to his father at a moment of relative calm and mutual tenderness in *Long Day's Journey Into Night*: "Stammering is the native eloquence of us fog people."[12] Similarly, it would be difficult to sum up more expressively the play's philosophy; the attitude, youth, and physical condition of Edmund; as well as the crippled condition of the entire family, than O'Neill does in:

> It was a great mistake, my being born a man, I would have been much more successful as a seagull or a fish. As it is, I will always be a stranger who never feels at home, who does not really want and is not really wanted, who can never belong, who must always be a little in love with death![13]

But here again the exception illustrates the rule; these magnificent poetic lines are atypical of American drama, as Mary McCarthy correctly states.

Nevertheless, she overstates her case when she claims that there is no poetry in American dramatic writing and subsequently asserts that American drama is, therefore, seriously defective. While narrowly and literally she is correct, the defect, if such it may be called, is less serious than she claims. In many American plays, the dialogue of the characters is appropriate and consistent, and this internal Aristotelian test of decorum and unity is of far greater consequence than any externally imposed judgment born of romantic sensibility or traditionalism, or even love of language per se.

To assess the dialogue of American drama as being only realistic–naturalistic, devoid of poetry and reflecting the base reality of a tape recorder, is neither accurate nor fair. Dialogue in the best American plays is selective dialogue, endowed with the pressure of experience and intensified and particularly activated by the richness of American idioms. In Edward Albee's *Virginia Woolf*, in which verbal nuance and phrasal gymnastics reach a level of literal poetry, the point need not be argued. But even in Arthur Miller's *Death of a Salesman*, in which the harried and unsuccessful Willy Loman proudly and repeatedly instructs his sons in the virtues of popularity and a good personal appearance, we have a vital, colloquial idiom that reflects irony and character, provides a dramatic rhythm, and heightens the drama's overall effect. In the following speech, Willy compares his boys with the studious Bernard, a neighbor's son:

> That's just what I mean. Bernard can get the best marks in school, y'understand, but when he gets out in the business world, y'understand, you are going to be five times ahead of him. That's why I thank Almighty God you're both built like Adonises. Because the man who makes an appearance in the business world, the man who creates personal interest, is the man who gets ahead. Be

liked and you will never want. You take me, for instance. I never have to wait
in line to see a buyer. "Willy Loman is here!" That's all they have to know, and
I go right through.[14]

It is more accurate, then, to say that the language of American drama
is quasi-poetic, resourcefully employing common speech patterns and
vocabulary for dramatic purpose.

This qualification, however, in no way detracts from the broader
application of Mary McCarthy's observation: a major characteristic of
mainstream American drama is the realistic–naturalistic mode of
dramatic dialogue, which, enriched by American idiom, reflects the
very essence of American culture. Just as Alphonse Daudet, in his
story "The Last Class," claimed language to be the essential
repository of a culture,[15] so dialogue must be considered at least a
powerful clue to the dramatic ethos of a nation. As Friedrich Durrenmatt argues, the word rather than the gesture is still the key element in
modern drama.[16] Antonin Artaud's diametrically opposite notion that
gesture provides the mimetic, primitive core of meaningful dramatic
experience[17] is too extreme. Language, itself a somewhat primitive
gesture, is profoundly interwoven with mimetic elements in drama.
Even if this were not so, the linguistic characteristics of plays would
still yield invaluable indices of the styles of both individual playwrights
and of individual nations and cultures. Specifically, the
realistic–naturalistic dialogue mode of American playwrights is not
simply a detached dramatic or theatrical element, but rather a primary
clue to American drama.

Our dramatic modes are indeed diverse—the rich expressionism of
Elmer Rice, the inventive, philosophically grounded surrealism of
Thornton Wilder, the seriously poetic intention of Maxwell Anderson,
and the numerous instances of hybridization. And in each instance,
these diverse modes are made powerful, imaginative, and exciting by
experiments in dialogue, movement, and nonverbal and/or actor-
oriented dramaturgy, particularly in those plays of the Third Theatre
and the later works produced in the East Village. However, the fact remains that the mainstream of our drama is, like our dialogue, a
realistic–naturalistic, artistic expression. Mary McCarthy has observed that our drama is journalistic, as if the playwright carried about
a tape recorder and a camera and gave us only a slightly amended ver-

sion of what his machines captured. Robert Brustein has criticized American theatre as lacking in a drama of ideas, asserting that it dwells on sexual matters in too unbridled and uncritical a fashion. Although both McCarthy's and Brustein's statements are exaggerations, it is true that the drama of ideas has not flourished in America as it has in Europe, as, for example, in the plays of Shaw and Ibsen; it is also true that poetic and surrealistic dramatic expression, particularly the darkly pessimistic varieties of such modes as Ionesco's and Beckett's, have not constituted the core of American drama.

For the most part, American dramatists have depicted realistic characters in rather familiar circumstances. The characters speak, dress, move, and act as we imagine most people do in daily life situations. Surely, the characters and situations possess a heightened intensity, but the intensity is subtly conveyed, immersed in the richly textured atmosphere of verisimilitude. The problems are perhaps more serious than those encountered by the masses and have more devastating (or, in comedy, more zany) results than are normal, but the "slice-of-life" drama of the United States is an almost uncomfortably accurate reflection of the striving, frustrations, concerns, and rhythms of the common man. We must emphasize, of course, that the terms *realism* and *naturalism*, just like *expressionism* or other artistic *-isms* are all descriptions of imaginative experience, which is both initially and ultimately grounded in the actualities of human experience, although transmuted by the creative processes of the artist's mind.

To cite the realistic–naturalistic mode as the dominant mode is to suggest a preponderance in number, not an exclusive excellence. One would indeed be hard-pressed to prove that the "slice-of-life" drama has artistically eclipsed the drama of social protest in America. During the 1930s our most distinguished drama was a literary outcry against social injustice; even today, in the work of such a playwright as Arthur Miller, it is difficult to designate a single dramatic category for the canon, since Miller intermingles the social protest strain so completely with his realistic–naturalistic bent. Similar observations may be made in regard to other playwrights; the element of social protest is indelibly ingrained in the expressionism of Elmer Rice, the surrealism and Absurdism of Albee, and the experimentalism of O'Neill. Even the psychological texture of Williams' and Inge's works is deeply colored by a commitment to changing and reforming American society.

In both the dominant realistic–naturalistic mode, with its emphasis upon the personal and, at times, the universal, and in the multi-modal social protest drama, at once group-oriented, temporal, and contemporary, there are certain subjects that recur more frequently than others. As might be expected, they are the same subjects that, thematically regarded, have stirred the creative fire of America's novelists. In 1968, Burton Feldman wrote, in an article entitled "Anatomy of Black Humor" in *Dissent*: "One can call Black Humor a literature of the academy even while admitting that it takes up the American novels' homely themes of sex, money, loneliness, and the rat race."[18] Such "homely themes," coupled with the destruction of dreams, constitute the major concerns of American drama. For example, *Death of a Salesman*, which is regarded by many as one of the most incisively American plays ever written, incorporates all of the subjects alluded to by Feldman. Through such concerns, the American dramatists have created a valuable reflectin of, and key to, the national ethos.

American drama, although written since the early days of our nation, did not flower until the twentieth century. It owes its maturation to the writing of Eugene O'Neill and, perhaps, to the dedication of Susan Glaspell and George ("Jig") Cram Cook, those imaginative idealists whose Provincetown Players first granted production—and such sensitive production—to O'Neill's early sea plays. American drama is marked by diversity, enriched by stubborn, tested hope, and—despite extensive experimentation, particularly in its drama of social protest—anchored in a realistic–naturalistic mode, in which essentially nonpoetic dialogue reaches levels of rare and moving intensity. Williams, Wilder, Inge, Miller, and Albee, all successors of O'Neill, share with him an international reputation. A partial list of other dramatists of stature in the twentieth century includes Elmer Rice, Philip Barry, Robert Sherwood, Maxwell Anderson, Lillian Hellman, Clifford Odets, S. N. Behrman, Neil Simon, Amiri Baraka, Jean Claude Van Itallie, Sam Shepard, David Rabe, Ed Bullins, John Guare, and Robert Anderson. Will any of these significant American dramatists emerge as the new O'Neill? Perhaps a new American dramatic genius exists. It is with high hope and anticipation, encouraged by examples such as the five plays discussed in this text, that we await the emergence of that individual.

Notes

[1]Alan Downer, "The Future of American Theater," *The American Theater Today* (New York: Basic Books, 1967), pp. 193-201.

[2]Arthur A. Nethercot, "The Psychoanalyzing of Eugene O'Neill," *Modern Drama*, December 1960, p. 242.

[3]Robert Brustein, *The Third Theatre* (New York: Simon and Schuster, 1958).

[4]Stuart W. Little, *Off Broadway: The Prophetic Theater* (New York: Coward, McCann and Geoghegan, 1972).

[5]Michael E. Rutenberg, *Edward Albee: Playwright in Protest* (New York: Drama Book Specialists, 1969).

[6]Martin Esslin, *The Theatre of the Absurd* (New York: Doubleday, 1961).

[7]Joseph Wood Krutch, *The Modern Temper: A Study and a Confession* (New York: Harcourt Brace, 1929), pp. 115-143.

[8]Mary McCarthy, "The American Realist Playwrights," *On the Contrary* (New York: Farrar, Strauss, and Cudahy, 1961), p. 305.

[9]Tennessee Williams, *The Glass Menagerie*, in *The Modern Theatre*, ed. Robert W. Corrigan (New York: Macmillan, 1964), p. 1238.

[10]Archibald MacLeish, "Arts Poetica," *The Human Season* (Boston: Houghton Mifflin, 1972), pp. 141-142, ll. 23-24.

[11]Eugene O'Neill, *Strange Interlude*, in *The Plays of Eugene O'Neill* (New York: Random House, 1955), p. 19.

[12]O'Neill, *Long Day's Journey into Night* (New Haven: Yale University, 1956), p. 154.

[13]*Ibid.*, pp. 153-154.

[14]Arthur Miller, *Death of a Salesman* (New York: Viking, 1949), p. 33.

[15]Alphonse Daudet, "The Last Class," *What Is the Short Story?*, ed. Eugene Current-Garcia and Walter R. Patrick (Chicago: Scott Foresman, 1961), p. 246.

[16]Friedrich Durrenmatt, "Problems of the Theatre," *Theatre in the Twentieth Century*, ed. Robert W. Corrigan (New York: Grove, 1963), p. 59.

[17]Antonin Artaud, "Preface," *The Theater and Its Double*, trans. Mary Caroline Richards (New York: Grove, 1958), p. 10.

[18]Burton Feldman, "Anatomy of Black Humor," *Dissent*, 15 (March/April, 1968), pp. 158-160.

Sticks
and
Bones

DAVID RABE

II

A Review of the Criticism

*D*avid Rabe's *Sticks and Bones*[1] joins his plays *The Basic Training of Pavlo Hummel* and *Streamers* to form a trilogy ostensibly concerned with military matters and the moral outrage of war.[2] Both *Sticks and Bones* and *Pavlo Hummel* were first professionally produced by Joseph Papp's Public Theater in 1971; as Mel Gussow informs us, it was the first time that the Public Theater had produced two plays by the same author simultaneously.[3] Subsequent to its off-Broadway run, the play was produced at Broadway's Golden Theatre, and an unauthorized version was presented at the Sovremennik Theater in Moscow.[4] Finally, after some delay and controversy, CBS aired the play on American public television.[5]

Written shortly after Rabe returned from service in Vietnam, *Sticks and Bones* is concerned with the return of a blind American war veteran to his home. Just as Rabe was struck by the indifference of his fellow citizens to the Vietnam experience, so David, the play's protagonist, finds himself morbidly out of step with his family, whose lives seem entirely unaffected by the war.

With certain notable exceptions, the critical reaction to David Rabe's *Sticks and Bones* has been extremely favorable. Among major critics, only Stanley Kauffmann and Walter Kerr have presented negative judgments. Henry Hewes, T. E. Kalem, Clive Barnes, Jack Kroll, John Donohue, Robert Berkvist, Brendan Gill, Catharine Hughes, and Harold Clurman have all praised *Sticks and Bones,* often with great enthusiasm. In general, they have praised Rabe's novelty of insight and expression; his seriousness and moral fervor; his perception, honesty, and intelligence; and his acumen as a satirist and analyst of American culture. While a few of these critics have disputed some of the positive comments of others, there has been relatively little negative criticism among his supporters.

Characteristic responses to the play include the following:

It is bitter and powerful, peppered with acrid humor and all the more disturbingly impressive on that account. (Clurman[6])

Occasionally in the theater one finds a play that drives deeper into the despair of existence than can be stated in clichés. [*Sticks and Bones*] . . . is invading with freshness and honesty some of the most painful ambiguities that afflict contemporary America. (Hewes[7])

While the territory he traverses is not new, Rabe strides across it with such intensity that the playgoer is raptly involved. (Kalem[8])

Sticks and Bones is a beautiful and harrowing study of American family life and American political life as a double nightmare from which only the most severely multilated among us struggle to awaken. (Gill[9])

Nothing in *Pavlo Hummel* prepared me for the dramatic intensity of *Sticks and Bones*. It has been a long time since I sat in an audience so moved and horrified by what went on in front of them. (Weales[10])

It is the best, the most powerful, certainly the most arresting drama currently to be seen on Broadway. (Hughes[11])

And the examples could be extended.[12]

What has been said of *Sticks and Bones* has been said also of Rabe as an American dramatist. Rarely has a playwright achieved such success so quickly, and the terms in which he has been praised have been extraordinary. Referring to Rabe's involvement with the Public Theater, Joseph Papp has said, "He is the most important writer we've ever had." Moreover, Papp has compared him to Eugene O'Neill because Rabe is "so painfully honest."[13] Catharine Hughes has suggested that "Rabe may well be the most impressive young American playwright to emerge since Edward Albee."[14] Similarly, Harold Clurman has called him "the most promising playwright,"[15] and Brendan Gill has referred to him as "already a formidable figure."[16] The list could easily be extended to include others who have used superlatives to acclaim this prize-winning young playwright.

The list, however, would not include Stanley Kauffmann, who is highly critical of *Sticks and Bones*, and believes that Rabe is one example of a group of recent American playwrights who have been vastly overrated by the critics. In separate reviews in 1971 and in 1973, he criticized not only the play, but Rabe's originality and usage. Although he asserts in the first review that the play is "considerably more interesting" than *Pavlo Hummel*, Kauffmann states that the best aspect of the play is its pop art mode: it swells trivia into threat, "spotlighting the frenzy with which coziness is defended."[17] What is wrong with the play is its "river of rhetoric," purple passages that Kauffmann believes are hardly worthy of an apprentice writer. Moreover, the play is built around trite, dull ironies: the blind man who can see, the sick "healthy people," the unchristian priest, the pure Vietnamese "whore," and so on. In essence, Kauffmann claims that "Rabe's vision is insufficient,"[18] and that his attack on the myopic middle classes is old hat. Despite all the flaws Kauffmann cites in this earlier review of *Sticks and Bones*, he still asserts that Rabe is a prospect to be watched for future development.

In the second review, however, Kauffmann expresses deep dissatisfaction over Rabe's development. He reaffirms his judgment that *Sticks and Bones* is a "mixed bag," and goes on to claim that Rabe's play *The Orphan* is "ludicrous," so bad that he refuses to review the play or the production. In essence, he blames the other critics for overpraising Rabe at the outset; he sees such exaggerated acclaim as a disservice to the playwright, and blames the critics for repeatedly overrating many other young artists whose work had some merit, but who hardly merited the claims made for them.[19]

Walter Kerr, although definitely more positive and hopeful about Rabe's future contributions, shares Kauffmann's dissatisfaction with *Sticks and Bones*. The headline of his review—"Unmistakably a Writer—Why, Then, Does His Play Stand Still?"—foreshadows his thesis that:

> Mr. Rabe is unmistakably a writer, though he remains a writer of detail that doesn't knot itself, or drive itself forward, into drama.
>
> *   *   *
>
> David comes home unapproachable, [and] remains unapproachable. We don't know [the precise reason or reasons for this hatred, and] the family begin as obtuse [and] remain exactly as obtuse as they were.[20]

Kerr and Kauffmann are in the minority, but they have argued forcefully.

Harold Clurman has called *Sticks and Bones* a "gross fantasy," and many other critics, whether praising or panning the work, have commented upon its fusing of naturalistic/surrealistic and comic/tragic elements. Many have also used the term *anti-war* to describe its theme (and the themes of other Rabe plays). Rabe objects to this formulation, although he admits that his Vietnam service was a profound influence on his work. As he states in an interview with Robert Berkvist:

> I don't like to hear them called anti-war plays. Works like that, like some of the social-action plays of the thirties, are designed for immediate effect. All I'm trying to do is *define the event* for myself and for the other people. I'm saying in effect, "This is what goes on" and that's all.[21]

More precisely, in an interview with Brendan Gill, Rabe has said: "There's a thematic connection between 'Pavlo' and 'Sticks'. . . since both are about the Vietnam war, but there's a moral connection, too—a connection of moral outrage."[22] Rabe has also interpreted his play as "a play about sophisticated tribalism in which ritual is used to define the insiders and outsiders of the tribe and make the definition hold."[23] He wrote this in his angry reaction to an attempt by Andrzej Wajda and the Moscow Sovremennik Theater to present the play as anti-American propaganda. Finally, in an interview with John Beaufort, prior to the CBS telecast version, Rabe commented that the play's major premise is that to many people "stubbing your own big toe is a more disturbing event than hearing of a stranger's suicide."[24]

Among the critical comments on the meaning of the play, Henry Hewes made a frank admission that probably reflects the feelings of many of his colleagues; he began his interpretation with the words, "Although I cannot fully comprehend its meaning. . . ." However, Hewes did venture a partial reading, and cited Rabe's honesty in explaining "some of the most painful ambiguities that afflict contemporary America."[25]

Other critics have also offered interpretations. Clive Barnes, for example, claims that *Sticks and Bones* displays many of the same concerns as *Pavlo Hummel*; it is especially concerned with what Vietnam (and, by extension, any other war) has done to the participants and what it reflects of their values and sensibilities. T. E. Kalem comments on the satire of the American culture:

> They [the members of the family] are hypocrites and moles. They are also a sad-funny, surreal-absurdist clan, whose like has not been seen on the U.S. stage since Edward Albee's *The American Dream*. The father is named Ozzie and the mother Harriet, which is a clue to the lowest level of the playwright's satiric intent and achievement.[26]

Also stressing the television symbolism, Gerald Weales comments: "Rabe is using the obvious fakery of television to question the reality of middle-class America, the behavioral empty shell that leads not simply to high Nielson ratings but to Mylai."[27]

In the view of his critics, then, Rabe is expressing outrage about what he exposes in America, both at war and in the living room. If we accept his contentions, perhaps he is exposing much more as well. Even with his own commentary and that of the critics, the precise meaning of the play is still a matter of conjecture. Is the play unclear? Is it truly a profound work that will permit many interpretations and never really yield an elementary, totally satisfying, all-encompassing truth? The many reviews and articles leave these questions unanswered.

A Discussion

Sticks and Bones was written by David Rabe in 1968, shortly after Rabe had completed his first draft of *Pavlo Hummel.* Actually, the playwright had alternated the writing and revisions of the plays, both of which are deeply concerned with our involvement in Vietnam. As its title implies, *The Basic Training of Pavlo Hummel* is concerned with the indoctrination of an Army recruit. Reflecting Pavlo's pre-Army life as a kid from the streets of New York, it surrealistically traces the period from his induction to his violent death in a Vietnam brothel. *Pavlo Hummel* was produced by Joseph Papp at the Public Theater in 1971.

Sticks and Bones, also produced by Papp at the Public Theater, was earlier presented at Villanova University in 1969. From the Public Theater, where it ran simultaneously with *Pavlo Hummel*, it went to Broadway. In 1972, it received the Tony Award for the Best Play on Broadway.

David Rabe has expressed dissatisfaction with those critics who term his works "anti-war plays," for he believes that such labeling is misleading and reductive. Moreover, he has expressed his own frustration in trying to interpret his plays:

> Most notions that occur to me as being possibly interpretive of these plays are met in my mind with disapproval. I don't know—or perhaps don't want to know—anything definitive, about them.[28]

Sticks and Bones tells of the return home of David, a young soldier blinded in Vietnam. Were this a conventional play, we might well expect the theme to concern itself with the adjustments of a handicapped veteran and his family. But such is not the focus. While the play is concerned with adjustment, it is not adjustment that results directly from the wound. Rather, it is the mental and emotional adjustment that David has made because of his war experience; it is his cultural ethos and spiritual vision that have changed, far more than his body and his physical vision. More precisely, Rabe employs David's physical condition and the new relationship with his family as a springboard for examining American values: the standards and assumptions by which we live, our motivation to go to war, what happens to those who go to war, the American ethos, and what hope we can have for the future.

In its biting social criticism, theatricality, and mixture of comedy and tragedy, *Sticks and Bones* is reminiscent of *America Hurrah*, one of the finest plays to be produced in America in the mid-sixties. It employs a familiar American cultural analogue, television's "Ozzie and Harriet," to project its vision. Since the Nelson family represented a typical, happy American family to millions of people, its use permits Rabe to make rather broad and piercing commentaries on America.

The familiar Nelson model might tempt us to assume that the play is simply a piece of national criticism; however, such an assumption would be incorrect. We learn this most trenchantly from Rabe's statements concerning the Soviet misuse of his play as anti-American propaganda; Rabe's letter to Andrzej Wajda states that if a bona fide interpretation of his play had been offered in Moscow, it would have been set in Russia, with the return of a Soviet soldier to his home; it would not have put exclusive emphasis on the shortcomings of American society.[29]

While Rabe's comment is helpful in defining the scope of *Sticks and Bones*, the play itself affords even better evidence of the breadth of his vision. Its very structure seems to fit more easily into the patterns of traditional tragedy than it does into those of the drama of social protest. In traditional tragedy, we often learn at the play's conclusion that a terrible blight had existed before the play's beginning. Sophocles' Oedipus, for example, learns only at the conclusion of the play that he has violated his mother and killed his father. However, he learns that such violation of primeval taboos was grounded in an ancient curse; action within the play had been destined by something that had existed long before the inception of action. Upon learning of his predestined situation, Oedipus blinds himself. Similarly, Ozzie and Harriet are not aware at the play's beginning of the blight at the heart of their lives. It is there, but they derive some dim awareness of it only at the play's conclusion. This awareness is dim indeed, for, incredibly, they do not ever entirely understand their plight. Unlike Oedipus, they are blind throughout the play and, comically and pathetically, they *remain* blind, even when reasonably sensitive and intelligent people would be shocked to awareness. Therefore, unlike Oedipus, Ozzie and Harriet lack the spiritual noblesse of classical tragic figures. In their obtuseness, they resemble Eliot's Sweeney or Swift's yahoos; they remain insensitive and unaware of their own condition. The habits of their lives, their American ethos, have so shielded them from truth that the significance of the trauma they experience in the play never gets through to them. This obtuse behavior surely exposes social flaw, but, grounded as the play is in traditional tragic structure and in the evocation of pain, it can hardly be described as simply a play of social protest. David's blindness at first seems to be the play's principal problem, but as the play moves on, we pierce further and further into the intangible darkness that lies beneath and around the superficial blindness. This deeper, intangible darkness is the horror of Joseph Conrad's Kurtz in *Heart of Darkness*; it is caused by a blindness that lies deeper than the physical blindness of David; it is the blindness of Eliot's "Hollow Men."

Rabe's use of prologue and epilogue is another pattern of traditional tragedy. In the prologue, Ozzie and Harriet are discovered watching old family slides; at the play's conclusion the slide technique is employed again. In the latter sequence only the face of David is shown, and this emphasis is crucial. David is identified as "Somebody sick" (p. 120) in both slide sequences. Symbolically, he is the sickness of the family, of the society, and perhaps of life itself. The prologue suggests that at nine years old he has already been infected; by the climax–epilogue, the meaning of David's sickness has been clarified. As Rabe suggests in his final comment on the slide, "it hovers, stricken, sightless, revealed" (p. 223).

To reinforce the play's tragic dimension, Ozzie is referred to in the first slide as "Grandpa Oswald." Oswald is the name of the blighted son in Ibsen's socio-tragic play, *Ghosts*. In that play, as Francis

Fergussen (*The Idea of a Theatre*) reminds us, Mrs. Alving is the tragic character, but her son Oswald, who has inherited the syphylitic blight from his father, is the symbol of the tragic core that infects and destroys the entire family.[30] It seems that one powerful ingredient of Rabe's art is his use of allusion to some of the richest plays of tragic theatre.

Following the slide prologue, we meet some of the principal characters. Ozzie, the father; Harriet, the mother; and Rick, David's brother. We also meet Father Donald, a clergyman who has been in the final slide with Ozzie and Harriet. It is that final slide that comes to life as Father Donald, who will later play a prominent part in the play, reveals his character. He is holding a basketball and speaking to Ozzie and Harriet of the need to provide young people with recreation, so they will not do anything antisocial. More specifically, he is trying to get Ozzie interested in playing on a team. With the self-important fervor, vacuous certainty, and high spirits of the evangelical salesman of religion, Father Donald attempts to explain away all human problems with overly simplistic answers.

This dynamic simplicity of Father Donald mirrors the spotless, television-comedy simplicity of the household, Ozzie's pride in his former prowess as a track star, and Rick's youthful enthusiasm for ice cream, cookies, fudge, and milk. Rick enters and shortly thereafter Father Donald leaves. The empty ritual of Rick's initial "Hi, Mom, hi, Dad" projects the whole empty, vapid, plastic atmosphere of the family.

During these opening minutes, the family talks of a person named Hank Grenweller. He apparently had much to do with the direction of Ozzie's life. He encouraged Ozzie to marry Harriet, he encouraged them both to buy the house in which they live, and both Ozzie and Harriet think of him as a kind of god. He was present at a family picnic about which Ozzie and Harriet reminisce, and his letting Ozzie beat him in a foot race was apparently one of the ways he managed to make Ozzie look good at a time when life was simpler, when Ozzie and Harriet's happiness was less challenged, and when Ozzie's self-image was building. Hank's role appears to have been that of the true middle-class hero of success: the good old boy who introduced Ozzie to Harriet, the successful businessman who kept in shape and remained a champion at work and on the athletic field. He was Ozzie's hero, and Ozzie has always wanted to emulate him, to catch his magic. Further, Ozzie would like his sons to emulate this demi-god. The fact that David never has, and that Rick has so little character at all, disturbs Ozzie; since Hank left, Ozzie has had no hero, no image to emulate, and no evidence in his sons of a new hero. The bestower and booster of male pride is gone. This disturbing loss is then compounded when Ozzie hears that Hank is diseased, literally rotting away. Ozzie's hero has not only left him, but has now disintegrated, in body and in image.

David has also left Ozzie and Harriet; perhaps, as an embarking soldier, he represented a new god to them. When Ozzie and Harriet learn that he is returning home, they are unaware of his injury. Implying confidence in happy endings, and specifically in the power of her prayers to bring him home safely, Harriet goes to bed, leaving Ozzie and Rick in the living room to greet David.

In the prologue we learn of sickness and of someone's dying of scarlet fever. Afterwards, we watch as Ozzie receives first a phone call with no speaker on the other end, and then a frightening call in which he is rudely asked his name by an Army official. In other words, some very negative ingredients have been exposed in this "typical" happy home. Then, as Rick and Ozzie speak, we learn that Ozzie worked in a defense plant during the last war and that he feels ashamed that he was not a fighter. He is glad that David showed a mean streak, a capacity to kill, even as a child. We also learn that Rick is somewhat jealous of David. Some things are, if not rotten, at least not quite all right in this typical American home.

With this ambiguous atmosphere established (the typical happy-home syndrome versus discontent and turmoil), we experience the shocking first episode in the play's central action, the return of David.

David, now blind, is brought home by a tough Army sergeant who speaks roughly to him and to the rest of the family. The sergeant speaks of a convoy of maimed and ill soldiers whom he is delivering all over the country; he speaks of them not as heroes but as damaged goods for which he is merely an overworked delivery service. David's first reaction, even before the sergeant leaves, is that he does not feel that he is at home. Symbolically, his war experience has made the home environment unreal to him. Even after he has heard their voices, he does not believe that these people are his family. He touches their faces for better recognition, but fearfully says to the sergeant, ". . . there's something wrong; it all feels wrong. . . . I don't know these people!" (p. 132).

When it is clear to David that he is at home, the rest of the act has to do with David's inability to settle back into things as they were and the inability of his parents and brother to establish a meaningful rapport with him. He lies awake, will not eat, resists the mollifications of his parents, speaks of the horrors of the war, spoils an attempt to raise his spirits by a party, mutters to himself, tells them about a Vietnamese woman he loved, and expresses guilt at having left her in Vietnam after she had shown him true love.

David's family reacts with increasing uncertainty and horror. His mother tries to give him food and sleeping pills. Both parents suggest that his discomfort is temporary. Harriet suggests going to church. Ozzie tries to assure David that he understands that war can be rough and that David's alleged whoring (Ozzie's interpretation) is understandable since men at war are often lonely and alone. Moreover, Rick shallowly accepts David back as if nothing at all has happened, and even tries to entertain him with silly songs over pretzels and potato chips.

The more David resists, the more his parents undergo stress. Particularly bothersome is David's suggestion that Hank Grenweller, the family friend, had a congenital disease of the face and hands. According to David, Hank visited him in California just before David went overseas. Ozzie is incredulous, but David insists that he saw Hank and that Hank is diseased. Since Hank is a godlike figure and a representative of the American ethos, the underpinnings of the family, David's assertion is terribly upsetting.

Also upsetting is David's revelation of his relationship with Zung, the Vietnamese woman. So upset is his mother that she literally vomits. His father is sufficiently upset to question his fathering of David, for whose existence he blames Harriet; Harriet blames David's problems on Ozzie's having taught him to play sports and to fight.

This mutual recrimination characterizes the family reaction to David, as do the continual relapses into familiar ideas and sayings, the constant pattern of departures from David and the house, and the self-questioning of Ozzie. Ozzie tells the story of his early life as a track star, his hopes for a materially satisfying future inspired by Hank, Hank's introducing him to Harriet, who evoked erotic feelings, and the whole pattern of loss of self and loss of meaning that has come to characterize his life. Ozzie begins to feel worthless and empty and angry, and Harriet becomes strident as her familiar role of food-giver and house-arranger fails to soothe and satisfy the family and to protect her from David's piercing insights and horrifying attitudes. Rick simply takes pictures of everyone. He's an outsider, with his long hair and guitar. Shallow, immature, and selfishly narrow in his concerns, Rick is unable to relate to anyone. He understands nothing and involves himself in nothing.

David finally declares his hatred of his parents and of Rick. The family simply does not understand what David has become and what the ugliness is at the core of their lives. Ozzie takes aspirins and anonymously calls the police to get them to do something about his son. Harriet, Rick, and Ozzie try desperately at the act's conclusion to find protection in crossword puzzles and rapid talk of baseball; but we know they are losing their grip and snatching onto what is familiar. Something is rotten in the household and in David, who has somehow found shortcomings in the all-American wholesomeness of the Nelson model. David is more virtuous than his fellow family members for he, at least, has reached through pain to some awareness of the truth; this vision of truth is partially a negative gaze at the tawdriness of the Nelsons' social existence, but, more profoundly, it is similar to "the horror of it all" of Conrad's *Heart of Darkness.*

Throughout this act, Zung has appeared surrealistically as a reminder to David of lost love and sensitivity; through Harriet's reaction, of the narrowness of middle-class prejudice; and of the horror of war itself. David, who feels extremely guilty at having left her, begs her to stay.

In the second act, the family repeatedly attempts to speak with David in order to calm him down and recapture the happy order of the household. Harriet suggests to Rick that he find David a nice girl, and brings Father Donald to speak with David. Both Harriet and Father Donald think that David's guilt over the alleged whoring constitutes his problem. Father Donald confidently enters David's room and suggests that David is in despair, which can only be eliminated by religion.

Father Donald, ethnocentric and ethically deficient in his faulty
assumption that David's alleged sexual experiences in Vietnam were illicit, tries awkwardly to soothe and bless him. But David swipes at the
shallow, hypocritical clergyman with his cane. Father Donald simply
leaves and stays far away, as Jesus does, according to Harriet.

When fudge-eating Rick goes to talk with David, he simply grins
and says, "Hi, David." When David returns "Hi, Rick," Rick accepts
this and tells the family that David is fine.

Later, Harriet enters to give David a sponge bath and to speak
with him. She still believes it is possible to recapture her happy family
by feeding them and giving them love. Just before entering David's
room, she has told Rick how, when she was a girl, she lifted a litter of
squealing kittens and made them calm and quiet. With David, however, she is not successful; he tells her how the Vietnamese girls are
made into whores and dwells exclusively on the horrors of the war. In a
symbolic rape of his prejudiced mother with his cane, he drives her
from the room despite her appeal to his sensitivity and his feelings for
Zung, in whose memory, Harriet defensively claims, he ought not to be
cruel.

When David tells his father that his (Ozzie's) life is meaningless,
Ozzie's desperation and self-questioning deepen. He had formerly
doubted his own worth and prowess as indicated by his excessive
dependence upon and glorification of Hank Grenweller, who had encouraged his adoption of a middle-class, bourgeois lifestyle, a style that
shrouded but never truly eliminated Ozzie's terrible self-doubts. Now,
David's criticism clearly exacerbates a pre-existing psychosocial problem of Ozzie's. To extricate himself, Ozzie characteristically dodges
the real problem and tries only to discredit David, the witness. David's
challenge affects both Ozzie and Harriet, and they both experience
spells of weakness and dizziness. Harriet is then appalled to learn that
Ozzie has called the police to spy on David. Ozzie wants David's teeth
checked and fingerprints taken to make certain that David is really
David.

Another device for showing Ozzie's desperation is the incident of
Ozzie being hit by an egg from a passing car. He addresses this event
by blaming David. He also recalls his old buddies who would have
taken care of the egg-throwers. Faced with a deepening crisis, and

lacking Hank, Ozzie is desperate for support. His defense is now irrational; David has exposed Ozzie's weakness, but Ozzie cannot attack the weakness, so he attacks the accuser instead. To Ozzie, David, not Ozzie's superficiality, is the villain. Therefore, he feels that David must have also caused the egg incident. Harriet, returning once again to her ridiculously superficial role as family soother, addresses the problem by making it go away; she merely cleans Ozzie's egg-stained jacket.

Ozzie hates his son David, blames his wife for tricking him into marriage and family life, and sees his son Rick as a shallow pool of ugliness. Moreover, even if he does not fully grasp the fundamental meaninglessness and confusion in his own life, he feels it keenly. For this reason, he brings in a stack of papers (supposedly bills), noting items and prices of all he owns. He distributes the papers to chairs representing members of the family; he sees in the papers a cumulative definition of the identity of each family member. Materialism is Ozzie's final buffer against the void.

With Harriet and Ozzie coming apart as their vapid, superficial American ethos is destroyed, David persists in his attack, forcing his family to welcome the dead of Vietnam into their home. David insists that Zung and all she represents must be welcomed and embraced by them. Ozzie strangles the surrealistic image of Zung. Then the family retreats once more into the familiar; Rick discusses a funny movie he has seen, and Harriet suggests that someone go for groceries.

As the family members feverishly seek to shield themselves psychologically through an exchange of banalities reminiscent of Ionesco's *The Bald Soprano*, Rick approaches David. Because his parents are literally sick with confusion and fear, Rick blandly suggests that David kill himself, picking up on Ozzie's earlier suggestion that he wished David were dead. Rick reminds him of how he decided to leave Zung and not bring her home to meet all the problems. David, calmer now for having imposed his war experience on the uninvolved and otherwise safe family, and deeply guilty over Zung, accepts the suicide notion. He proceeds with the aid of his family—his mother brings silver pans and towels with roosters on them—to slit his wrists with Rick's razor.

Everyone is made happier by David's doing this. Ozzie, who has once again become head of the household, commands David to remove his glasses. Symbolically, the family can now adjust to the painful sight of David's face and wound. In so doing, they can turn from the deeper truth of what his (and their own) blindness really signifies. Everyone pretends that David will not die—he will only "nearly die," as Ozzie says. Rick suggests that David take a shower and put on clean clothes, and the play ends with his playing the guitar for David. Rabe's stage direction notes:

> The music is alive and fast. It has rhythm, a drive of happiness that is contagious (p. 223).

Symbolically, the family is returning to its old ways, having learned little from the experience through which they have lived.

Sticks and Bones, with its keen sensitivity to the venality of American society, is a savage satire of middle-class shallowness, smugness, and spiritual deficiency, and a pessimistic vision of the hellish condition of human beings on this earth. The play suggests that America's artificiality and superficiality lead us to narrow, ethnocentric behavior, to stonelike insensitivity, to savage and monstrous mistreatment of others, to the distortion of our lives, and to a condition in which death is better than life. The model from which this social criticism and existential pessimism is projected is a famous American television family, and the central event is the return from Vietnam of their wounded son, David. David drives his family to discover the ugliness and emptiness in their own lives, an ugliness and emptiness that, during the Vietnam era, caused devastation of a foreign land and the maiming of America's youth.

At one point in the play David says:

> Do you know how north of here, on farms, gentle loving dogs are raised, while in the forests, other dogs run wild? And upon occasion, one of those that's wild is captured and put among the others that are tame, bringing with it the memory of when they had all been wild—the dark and terror—that had made them wolves (p. 214).

This image accentuates what actually happens to the Nelsons. David, now a wild human, has been put back among his tame family members. He, more than camera-wielding Rick, takes a picture of his family, forcing them to see the emptiness, worthlessness, falsehood, and cruelty of their lives (i.e., their wolflike state) and to consider as well the essential chaos of life itself. Hank Grenweller, a god–devil, lures all of them to look for happiness in marriage, materialism, and family life; but this grinning improver (his name onomastically regarded) is only an illusion of hope and meaning. Like a number of American plays, *Sticks and Bones* almost seems to play out ritually its violence on American culture because the deeper mystery that that culture avoids and obscures is ultimately unfathomable and too terrible to contemplate without adulteration.

Many critics have admitted difficulty in discussing this play; indeed, it is a difficult work to describe, paraphrase, and analyze satisfactorily. It is explosive; like a poem, its verbal and theatrical images are so associatively and spontaneously presented that it resists simple, direct retelling. Its essence lies in the dynamic interplay of word, stage action, and theatrical resource (props, lighting, costumes, etc.). However, its mixture of the savagely brutal, the hilariously funny, the softly poetic, the pointedly critical, and the darkly pessimistic clearly conveys Rabe's vision of human loneliness in a universe without meaning and of a hellish American ethos, where people destroy love for security, beauty for plasticity, freedom for material wealth, and humane feeling for petty satisfactions of group affiliation. David Rabe has written a major work of dramatic art: it is little wonder that he has been called the "best young playwright since Edward Albee," someone to be compared favorably, according to the critic John Simon, with America's greatest dramatist, Eugene O'Neill.[31]

Entwining of the Strands

While the realistic dimension of *Sticks and Bones* is interwoven with its surrealistic counterpart throughout the play, the realism can be somewhat distinguished, albeit imperfectly, from the play's other major strain.[32] The elucidation of this distinction is crucially important in any critical response to the play, for it is the play's realism that creates an emotional framework for our responses, provides a background for the starkly contrasting Absurdist strain, and lures us, through its familiarity, toward the frightening and enlightening perceptions that inform the vision of this poetic work.

Realistically regarded, the play centers on the return of a blind Vietnam veteran to his middle-class American family. The other family members are a father, a mother, and a younger brother. The family is of average size and carries the familiar Nelson name, permitting Rabe to suggest profitably and pointedly that it is typically American. As a typical model, the Nelson family unit enables Rabe to make a powerful social protest statement, while at the same time it provides a familiar environment for the play's action and a possible foundation for its existential thrust. The family lives in a house with recognizably familiar decor, furniture, and such functional items as a phone, doorbell, television, etc. The people's relationships—husband–wife and parent–child—are believable in terms of mores and values, dialogue, and superficial behaviors. The sense of a shared past; the subtle and intimate knowledge of each other's habits; the individual recognition of family membership in a believably delineated local, national, and international environment; the fears and jokes; the pleasures and pains; the frustrations, angers, and manipulations; and the mutual concerns all serve to suggest that these are real individuals living real lives in a real American family.

The superficial realism of the individuals' personalities and characters, the realistic group interactions, the realistic intra- and extramural environment, and the essentially realistic crisis of the returning wounded son invoke our concern. Objectively regarded, the crisis develops as follows: a boy returns to his home, having been blinded in Vietnam and having left behind a girl with whom he had fallen in love. The physical injury and the loss of love are upsetting to him, but not nearly so upsetting as his experience of the brutality of war and his awareness of the fundamental emptiness and decadence of the society that sent him off to fight. In such a physical and emotional state, he returns to his family and upsets them terribly. Not only are they surprised by his physical condition, but they simply cannot understand or effectively respond to the new and profound attitudes—the anger and disillusionment—of the wounded soldier. At first, they expect that his behavior will change and become familiar and normal once more, so they do all they can to accept his behavior as a merely temporary discomfort. They pamper him; they try to talk to him; they disregard his intensity. When that does not work, they seek the help of a family friend, a priest; however, he, too, is unable to reach the young man. Totally at a loss as to how to reach him, and distraught and confused, they make the suggestion that the young man commit suicide in order that they themselves may survive.

The suicide suggestion is the culmination of the motif of denial and illusion-clinging that characterizes the family's response to the soldier and to what he says, does, and represents. In the context of the family's defensive reaction, the suicide suggestion seems psychologically understandable (and, therefore, realistic). However, it is clearly an extreme gesture, an absurd response to an absurd condition, with which neither the soldier nor the family can effectively contend. At its climax, then, the play merges the realistic and the Absurd so effectively that it is nearly impossible for us to maintain the distinction.

Actually, the strands of Absurdism and realism are intertwined from the play's opening scene; the consequent surrealistic distortions of the realistic details constitute the play's principal aesthetic thrust. More simply stated, the play never allows us to relax with the familiar. Instead, every detail and every scene is informed by Rabe's atoms of intensification—verbal and theatrical emphases—that lift his play beyond the realm of photographic description, beyond even the boundary of social protest, to a realm of fundamental existential perception.

The fact that the family is a serio-comic pop art rendering of a well-known, decidedly innocuous situation-comedy family tells us right away that Rabe is not interested primarily in photographic realism. Instead, the accumulation of the familiar, realistic details and the caricaturing (especially of Rick, with his "Hi," his fudge, and his guitar playing) tend to make us see the realistic details for what they are: a facade, a cover for a more serious and penetrating look at American culture, and also, as we slowly discover, a clue to a dark and unfriendly void that lies beneath the social superficialities and remains unfathomed by the mass of our people.

Through episodic plotting, poetic statement, blatant symbolism (the blindness, Ozzie's running, and Rick's fudge), and such expressionistic techniques as the appearance of Zung, Rabe suggests the materialistic decadence and selfish, ethnocentric cruelty of our culture, and the lonely, despairing condition of humans on this earth. As we watch David hack through the surfaces of his family's American dream, we realize, as the family members almost do themselves, that the ugly culture hides an even uglier chaos beneath. Our cruelties (Vietnam, prejudice, insensitivity, lies) are what we use to hide ourselves from the void that we fear, that we deny, but that we know to exist at the core of our lives.

Essentially, then, the blind David is both the blight that, like Oswald Alving in Ibsen's *Ghosts*, lies at the heart of existence and the seer who, like the blind Tiresias of Sophocles' *Oedipus Rex*, brings us the knowledge of the existence of that void.

Like Jean Claude Van Itallie in *America Hurrah*, Rabe cries out in savage tones against the ugliness of American culture, indeed of all Western culture. But Rabe goes on to project a truly poetic reflection of the dark, lonely condition of human beings; a condition in which materialism, war, ethnocentricity, and mass culture are the means—ugly and terrible—of selfish survival in the face of the void. Brilliantly, Rabe has fused episodic incident and linear plot, associative image and cause and effect development, poetry and prose, monologue and dialogue, comic and tragic impulses, in order to reveal a panorama of truths about American culture and about life and death itself. In *Sticks and Bones*, the intertwining of realistic and Absurdist aesthetic impulses is so effective and complete that we can hardly disentangle the rich linkage without distorting the delicately wrought dramatic arabesque Rabe has created.

Notes

[1]David Rabe, *Sticks and Bones* (New York: Viking Press, 1973). All pages cited are from this edition.

[2]*Pavlo Hummel*, the first of the trilogy to be produced, brought Rabe the "most promising [off-Broadway] playwright" citation of *Variety*'s poll of drama critics, an Obie Award, and the Hull-Warriner Award for best play on a controversial subject. *Sticks and Bones* won an Outer Circle Award and a Tony Award for best Broadway play of the 1971-1972 season, and brought Rabe *Variety*'s citation as "most promising new [Broadway] playwright." *Time* magazine (January 7, 1980, p. 97) selected *Sticks and Bones* as one of the ten best dramatic offerings of the 1970s. *Streamers* won the New York Drama Critics' Award for best American play of the 1975-1976 season.

³Mel Gussow, "2d David Rabe Play to Join *Pavlo Hummel* at Public Theater," *The New York Times*, 3 November 1971, p. 43.

⁴Rabe, "Each Night You Spit in My Face," *The New York Times*, 18 March 1973, II, pp. 3, 20. For the Soviet theater's response, *see*: Hedrick Smith, "Soviet Sticks and Stones for David Rabe," *The New York Times*, 12 April 1973, p. 56. *See also*: George Gent, "Rabe Protests Pirated Version of *Sticks and Bones* in Moscow," *The New York Times*, 13 March 1973, p. 31; and Henry Popkin, "How did *Sticks and Bones* fare in Moscow?," *The Christian Science Monitor*, 26 May 1973, p. 14.

⁵John Beaufort, "Controversial drama will air tomorrow after being vetoed," *The Christian Science Monitor*, 16 August 1973, p. 16. For background news on the controversy, *see*: John Beaufort, "Can stage buck success?," *The Christian Science Monitor*, 3 March 1973, pp. 123, 125; "CBS drops Viet drama," *The Christian Science Monitor*, 8 March 1973, p. 10; and Beaufort, "Television Pressures from 50's to 70's," *The Christian Science Monitor*, 24 March 1973, p. 24.

⁶Harold Clurman, "Theatre," *The Nation*, 22 November 1971, p. 539.

⁷Henry Hewes, "Only Winter Is White," *Saturday Review*, 27 November 1971, p. 70.

⁸T. E. Kalem, "Air-Conditioned Hell," *Time*, 22 November 1971, p. 93.

⁹Brendan Gill, "Real Play, False Play, No Play," *The New Yorker*, 11 March 1972, p. 82.

¹⁰Gerald Weales, "The Stage," *Commonweal*, 10 March 1972, p. 15.

¹¹Catharine Hughes, "An American Nightmare," *America*, 18 March 1972, pp. 294–295.

¹²For reviews by the other critics mentioned, *see*: Clive Barnes, "Theater: A Most Gifted Playwright," *The New York Times*, 8 November 1971, p. 53; Jack Kroll, "Theater," *Newsweek*, 29 November 1971, p. 100, and 20 December 1971, pp. 53, 61; John Donohue, "*Sticks and Bones* on TV," *America*, 1 September 1973, p. 120; and Robert Berkvist, "If You Kill Sombody . . . ," *The New York Times*, 12 December 1971, II, pp. 3, 22.

¹³Gussow, p. 43.

¹⁴Hughes, p. 295.

¹⁵Clurman, p. 539.

¹⁶Gill, p. 82.

¹⁷Stanley Kauffmann, "*Sticks and Bones*," *The New Republic*, 4 December 1971, p. 22.

¹⁸*Ibid.*

¹⁹Kauffmann, "Stanley Kauffmann on Theater," *The New Republic*, 26 May 1973, p. 22.

²⁰Walter Kerr, "Unmistakably a Writer—Why, Then, Does His Play Stand Still?," *The New York Times*, 14 November 1971, II, p. 3.

²¹Berkvist, p. 3.

[22]Gill, "Rabe," *The New Yorker*, 20 November 1971, p. 48.

[23]Rabe, "Each Night," p. 3.

[24]Beaufort, "Controversial drama will air . . . ," p. 16.

[25]Hewes, p. 70.

[26]Kalem, p. 93.

[27]Weales, p. 15.

[28]Rabe, "Introduction," *The Basic Training of Pavlo Hummel and Sticks and Bones* (New York: Viking Press, 1973), p. ix. All pages cited are from this edition.

[29]Rabe, "Each Night," p. 3.

[30]Francis Fergussen, *The Idea of a Theatre* (Princeton: Princeton University Press, 1949), p. 166.

[31]John Simon, "Domestic Infernos," *New York* 4:47 (22 November 1971), p. 76.

[32]The Theatre of the Absurd possesses certain dominant characteristics: (1) non-linear plotting; (2) associative rather than causal dramatic development; (3) nightmarish atmosphere; (4) an emphasis on mimetic elements rather than language as a reliable and effective means of communicating and reflecting the Absurdist life view; (5) an intermixture of comic and noncomic elements; and (6) a dark, negativistic life philosophy. These ingredients in relation to each other—and to certain minor technical and conceptual motifs—constitute, allowing of course for an individual playwright's stylistic differences, this rich dramatic expression. While Absurdism as a style and a philosophy can be discerned sporadically in portions of the works of our greatest dramatists (Shakespeare, for example, in *King Lear*), the Theatre of the Absurd is essentially a post-World War I dramatic type.

In order to convey his Absurdist vision, the Absurdist writer must, of course, borrow and rely upon such traditional dramatic modes as farce, comedy, presentational theatrical approaches, expressionistic externalization of the intangible, the whole range of surrealistic possibilities, and even poetic drama. Clearly, these traditional modes were not the invention of the Absurdist dramatist; assuredly they should not be directly credited to Pinter, Ionesco, Beckett, Genet, or other Absurdists.

Although these modes are not specifically Absurdist (sometimes they are even employed in the service of realism), they are, nevertheless, often, in fact usually, an integral part of an Absurdist work. For this reason, I have, where appropriate, attempted to indicate the particular reliance of a particular Absurdist play on one or more of these traditional modes. In no way do I mean to suggest an equation of Absurdism with any one or even all of these expressions; Absurdism, as indicated, has an aesthetic and an ethos all its own. However, I do believe that the Absurdism of a particular play is often realized through an indebtedness and even an actual reliance upon one or more of these modes.

The House of Blue Leaves

JOHN GUARE

III

A Review of the Criticism

*J*ohn Guare's *The House of Blue Leaves* won the New York Drama Critics' Circle Award as the best American play of the 1970–1971 season. Guare's previous play, *Muzeeka*, won an Obie in 1968; in 1970 another work, *Cop-Out*, earned him the title of "Most Promising Playwright" in *Variety*'s poll of New York drama critics. Following *The House of Blue Leaves*, he collaborated on a musical adaptation of Shakespeare's *Two Gentlemen of Verona*, which won the New York Drama Critics' Circle Award as the Best Musical of 1971–1972. Several additional Guare plays have been produced, including *Rich and Famous* (1976), *Marco Polo Sings a Solo* (1977), *Landscape of the Body* (1977), and *Bosoms and Neglect* (1979). It is little wonder that Henry Hewes has stated, "Of all the new American playwrights to emerge in the last decade, the most successful is John Guare."[1]

According to Patricia Bosworth, who interviewed Guare, he got the idea for *The House of Blue Leaves* in 1965, at the time Pope Paul VI came to New York. Traveling in Rome, Guare began to imagine his parents' probable preparations for and reactions to the Pope's visit. Guare describes his parents as unhappy, bright, isolated people. Their condition and behavior and a number of specific events in his own life combine to create the fabric of the work. Although critics pro and con describe the play as "zany" and "bizarre," the extent of Guare's autobiographical involvement and identification is revealed by his concluding remark to Ms. Bosworth in the interview:

> You know the only difference between me and those looney lost characters in *The House of Blue Leaves*? Nobody ever said "yes" to their fantasies. Thank God, somebody finally said "yes" to mine.[2]

Although the play is allegedly deeply autobiographical, the surface events are entirely fictional. As Harold Clurman says, "The central figure of *The House of Blue Leaves*, Artie Shaughnessy, a man who tends animals in a zoo, has wanted all his life to be a pop songwriter."[3] A somewhat fuller description is provided by Julius Novick, who writes:

> The . . . new play takes . . . place on Oct. 4, 1965, the day the Pope came to New York, and concerns a zookeeper named Artie Shaughnessy. Artie's wife, Bananas Shaughnessy, is an hysterical lunatic, and Artie is in love with his downstairs neighbor, Bunny Flingus; he wants to elope with Bunny to Hollywood and become a songwriter. Artie's son Ronnie is a soldier, AWOL from Fort Dix or someplace like that, who dresses up as an altar boy in order to blow up the Pope."[4]

Farce is the primary mode of expression and, as the critics attest, social criticism is a major ingredient. The centrality of this social protest element is described by Edith Oliver in her *New Yorker* review: "[Guare] can be seen monkeying around with a variety of American dreams, circa 1965, as they afflict and finally destroy a middle-aged keeper at the Central Park Zoo who has a knack for imitating cheap Tin Pan Alley songs."[5] Henry Hewes reiterates with: "Guare has personified in Artie the American dream of success and the destructive forces unleashed by the frustration of never achieving it."[6] And Harold Clurman somewhat more directly asserts:

> Guare is not simply a prankster. What motivates him is scorn for the fraudulence of our way of life.[7]

Finally, in his interview with Patricia Bosworth, Guare himself gives support to those who detect a strong strain of social criticism in the work:

> Catholicism and show biz. So full of dreams and phoney promises. I started fusing them together in *House of Blue Leaves*, and when I did, I began to understand a little more about where I came from and why I am—peculiarly—the way I am.[8]

In addition to this social criticism and the interwoven autobiographical dimension Guare suggests, Clive Barnes has found a more universal, existential aspect to the play. He notes: "I laughed a great deal, and I recommend the play, yet I suspect that beneath the idiot laughter and the cruel jokes we are intended to feel compassion for the world's lost."[9] In discussing the play's genre, Guare himself seems to suggest that the play has a universal dimension that runs parallel to the social and psychological strains:

I chose farce because it's the most abrasive, anxious form and I'm trying to ex-
tend its boundaries because I think the chaotic state of the world demands it.
Who says I have to be confined and show a guy slipping on a banana peel? Why
can't I take him to the next level and show him howling with pain because he's
broken his ass?[10]

Yet one more testimony to the breadth of Guare's vision is afforded by
Julius Novick, who, like Barnes, found the play somewhat disturbing
and perceived a tragic strain beneath the play's superficial chaos:

It's easy to conjecture what Mr. Guare might be trying to do. The zany irrationality of farce colliding sharply and constantly with real pain—the laughter
that freezes on the lips—the confusion about how we're supposed to react—the
sense of exasperation and cross-purposes—what better way to body forth a vision of the Absurdity (if you can bear to see that word in print yet once again)
now commonly attributed to the human condition?[11]

Zany comedy and serious purpose seem to be the poles of Guare's
aesthetic substance in *The House of Blue Leaves*. Critics (both pro and
con) agree upon this. In fact, Patricia Bosworth has referred to it as a
"slapstick tragedy."[12] Yet it is this union of farce and anguish that has
received the greatest amount of critical commentary and that has
separated critics in their overall judgment of the play's quality. Walter
Kerr, Edith Oliver, and Henry Hewes praise the play; Clive Barnes,
Harold Clurman, and Julius Novick find it unsatisfying.

Novick's review, entitled, "Very Funny—Or a Long Sick Joke?,"
presents the most complex criticism. Novick finds the play highly
original and sees it as black comedy, in which laughter-producing
techniques are used to rub in pain. However, Novick argues that unlike
other writers of black comedy, Guare fails to filter the agony. He "goes
for broke," pouring the agony on full force with the "maddest, zaniest,
most physical farce." "Theoretically," Novick observes, "there's no
absolute reason why it couldn't work, and at moments I guess it does."
But Novick believes that on the whole it does not work; Guare does not
allow us to acknowledge our pain through our laughter; rather, he asks
us to deny the reality of the pain that is being so forcefully presented to
us. In so doing, he tries to lure us into laughing directly at human
misery. In Novick's view, this is inhumane and makes the play "a long
sick joke."[13]

Harold Clurman agrees with Novick that the comedy and anguish
are at odds, but he sees the play's failure in terms that are almost
diametrically opposed to those of Novick. Clurman believes that the
sadness mars the comedy. Not only is there a discrepancy of style, but

there is also an ingredient of cruel sorrow, epitomized in Bananas, which mars the fun and ultimately destroys the coherence of the play.[14] Clive Barnes, somewhat more ambivalent than either Clurman or Novick, criticizes the play for its "shapelessness." He feels that the play is so concerned with "despair" that it remains chaotic and its humor fails to scourge us. Although Barnes compliments Guare for his artful, "macabre zaniness," the play's comic thrust merely amuses,and thus it neither affects us deeply nor makes a significant commentary.[15] Although Barnes's analysis leaves certain matters unresolved, he seems to agree with Novick and Clurman that Guare has not successfully harmonized the elements of comedy and agony.

The critics who laud the play hold a precisely opposite view. Walter Kerr cites Guare's "exceptional gift for the bizarre phrase, antic gesture, [and] improbable stage picture," and states: "What is most impressive about the charade, for all its frayed edges, is that its greatest extravagances somehow reinforce the real pain at its center."[16] Henry Hewes agrees, stating: "Modern life may be best dramatized by viewing its horrors and its misery in comic terms. . . . Guare's comic facility is inextricable from an utter and moving emotional sincerity."[17] Edith Oliver, who, like other critics, cites the intermixture of genres, states:

> Mr. Guare has built a savage farce around a very sad story indeed. . . . Actually, this play could be considered a whole series of shock treatments, and often I was as horrified at myself for laughing (which I did a lot) as I was at what I saw and heard on the stage. The plot, as is true of the plots of all good farces, is wild, arbitrary, and dependent on outrageousness for its effect.[18]

Caprice and long windedness are flaws found by all three affirmative critics; Walter Kerr even states that Guare "doesn't know when to shut up."[19] However, such flaws do not keep them from evaluating the play in superlatives. Oliver calls Guare "a born playwright and satirist" and the play "valuable."[20] Hewes says he finds himself "valuing it more highly than any new play this season."[21] Kerr, who missed the play originally, cites it as "the most striking new American play of the season."[22]

Although Edith Oliver readily accepts the arbitrariness of the play as characteristic of the genre, Clive Barnes, as noted earlier, defines the arbitrariness as "shapelessness" and considers it a serious flaw.

Actually, this matter of structure is one with which Guare has tried to cope for some time. While Guare studied with John Gassner at the Yale School of Drama, he consistently rejected "the then prevalent emphasis on logic and good construction" and continued to do so when he studied with Arnold Weinstein. Guare believed that such disregard of established structure permitted him to open himself up. Later he realized that this free-spirited method allowed him to write only short works.[23] "So," in Henry Hewes' words, "he resolved to find a happier balance between getting deeper into himself and the problem of structure."[24] As for *The House of Blue Leaves*, he rewrote the second act of the play nine times until he was able to get the characters to interact to his satisfaction.[25] One wonders, therefore, whether Clive Barnes is correct in calling the play shapeless, or even whether the arbitrary quality noted and accepted by Edith Oliver is really present. It may be that the play's seemingly arbitrary surface conceals an inner coherence of consistent mood, dynamics, and vision, if not incident.

A Discussion

John Guare's two-act play *The House of Blue Leaves* was produced in 1971 in New York by Joseph Papp. The backdrop of the play is the 1965 visit of Pope Paul VI to New York City; the play's central action surrealistically depicts a brief period in the life of Artie Shaughnessy, a forty-five-year-old Queens resident who works as a zookeeper but dreams of being a Hollywood songwriter. The Queens setting is significant to Guare; in a foreword to the Viking edition of the play, he describes Queens as a borough without a clear and separate identity and a place of dreams that are often unfulfilled. According to Guare, the play's subject is humiliation, which he sees as the stuff of comedy and tragedy, and the core of our lives. This personal, autobiographical play is a transformation and collage of much of John Guare's actual and imaginative life; he dedicates it to his parents, with whom he feels he remained too long.[26]

Before the curtain rises, the audience sees Shaughnessy perform his songs at the El Dorado Bar and Grill. The house lights then fade, and the body of the play begins, focusing on the brief period of shortly before the Pope's visit to a few weeks later when Artie kills his wife, Bananas. Through the highly imaginative prologue at the El Dorado, one facet of the world of Artie Shaughnessy is vividly conveyed to the audience. Even before people have been seated, Artie comes out on stage and says nervously, "My name is Artie Shaughnessy and I'm going to sing you songs I wrote" (p. 3). And this is precisely what Artie proceeds to do. As we wonder whether the play is actually beginning, we watch and listen as he plunges into bad pop songs, calls for the blue spotlight promised him, and nervously runs off stage after completing a few numbers. Aesthetic distance has been broken by his direct address and by the spontaneity of the opening. Later we learn that this performance is part of a local talent show, to which Artie has gone with pathetically urgent hopes of being discovered. He does not find success, and he even has to buy his own beers. Thus, the prologue, retrospectively regarded, exposes Artie's frantic dream and lack of lyrical muse.

In Act I the scene shifts to Artie's Queens apartment, and we get a fuller picture of his world and the characters who share it. Artie's wife, Bananas, has suffered a mental breakdown and behaves very peculiarly. Artie has a mistress, Bunny Flingus, who lives downstairs. Guare's stage direction describes her as:

> . . . a pretty, pink, slightly plump, electric woman in her late thirties. She wears a fur-collared coat and plastic booties. . . (p. 11).

Ronnie, Artie's eighteen-year-old son, has been drafted into the Army, but is AWOL and hides in his bedroom throughout much of the play.

When we first encounter Artie, he is fast asleep in a sleeping bag on the living-room couch. Pictures of movie stars and jungle animals hang on the living-room walls; a piano is upstage center, littered with sheet music and manuscript paper. Artie dreams aloud that Ronnie, transformed into "Pope Ronald the First," has come to New York. As Artie sleeps, the real Ronnie, dressed in Army fatigues, climbs in a window, sneaks through the living room, takes bread and milk from the kitchen, and goes stealthily into his bedroom. Suddenly Artie is awakened by the doorbell, and his mistress, the energetic Bunny Flingus, enters. She is filled with excitement over the forthcoming arrival of the Pope and urges Artie to come out with her to view the motorcade on Queens Boulevard so that both of them can be blessed by His Holiness.

Bananas enters, but remains unnoticed by Artie and Bunny. Guare's stage direction describes her as "a sick woman in a nightgown" (p. 16). A later stage direction completes her characterization this way:

> She's lived in her nightgown for the last six months. She's in her early forties and has been crying for as long as she's had her nightgown on. She walks uncertainly, as if hidden barriers lay scattered in her path (p. 22).

Bunny continues to urge Artie to seek the Pope's blessing. It will be a new beginning for them. They will marry and go to Hollywood, where Artie will be a successful songwriter. She believes in Artie's talent and impending fame; she has spotted other hit songs, and knows that Artie's "Where Is the Devil in Evelyn?" is going to be a classic. After all, she "didn't work in Macy's Music Department for nix" (p. 16). She urges Artie to get in touch with his old friend, Billy Einhorn, now a Hollywood moviemaker; surely Billy will give Artie the break he needs.

Bananas throws Bunny's coat into the corridor and begins to bark like a dog. She speaks directly to the audience, welcoming us to her home. She then sneaks up behind Bunny and scares her with a red mask. Bunny complains that Bananas is emitting poison fumes from her sick head and confronts Artie about a Mexican divorce. Bunny and Artie tell Bananas that they plan to put her in a hospital and go off to California. Artie, encouraged by Bunny, calls Billy Einhorn and is elated that he and Bunny will see Billy "soon." Although Bananas complains that she cannot see the Pope because her "fingernails are all different lengths," she gets dressed and all three leave to see the Pope. After everyone has left, Ronnie emerges from his room carrying a large box. He walks downstage and stares at the audience as the curtain falls on the first act. The tension and mystery in Ronnie's actions accentuate the theatrical quality of the play.

The first act clearly reveals that this is no simple story of frustrated lives. Rather, the frustrations of the Shaughnessy family are symbolic of the frustrations imposed by the American dream of wealth and success, especially in New York, The Big Apple. Bunny's identification of the Pope's visit with the Taylor–Burton *Cleopatra* and the quasi-deificaton of Billy Einhorn (his name suggestive of the mythical unicorn) tell us that the American dream is both terrible and pernicious, dressed in glitter and orchestrated with Hollywood showmanship. We cannot realize that dream, and the pursuit leaves us exhausted, mad, and eternally unfulfilled.

We know from the outset that Bananas is quite ill. Prior to his call to Billy Einhorn, Artie gently mentions to her a "nice" hospital, a "house of blue leaves" (p. 32); actually, near the hospital there is a tree that, when filled with birds, resembles a tree with a canopy of blue leaves. When the birds are frightened, however, they fly away, and the tree's branches become bare. The blue leaves, the play's core image, suggest the illusion beneath which lies hard reality. There is no escape for Bananas in a house of blue leaves, though Artie tells her it is a place where she will get well.

So zany is Bananas' behavior in the play that she, pathetic as she is, also has a comic dimension to her. When she first interacts with Artie, she becomes hysterical and he gives her pills. She complains about the pills; they do not allow her to express her emotions. However, Artie must administer the medicine because her emotions are, as she aptly describes them, like caged animals, and they cannot be allowed to roam unchecked in the household. Later, when she eats, we see her acting hysterically again, pretending to be an animal and rolling around on the floor to be fed. This is perhaps her way of trying to win Artie's love, for she can no longer do so as a human being, even though she shares Bunny's enthusiasm for Artie's songs. Because Artie is a zookeeper, the animal behavior is symbolically appropriate.

We learn from later conversation (pp. 51–52) that Bananas has engaged in rather extreme actions twice before. Once she tried to kill herself by slitting her wrists. The other time, she left the house in a snowstorm and did not return for twenty-four hours. Ironically, she did not get sick, but Artie got pneumonia. Long ago the couple had had fun and had loved each other; through Billy, we hear of a happier past when Bananas was mentally healthy and the Shaughnessys shared good times with Billy and his wife, Georgina. However, as Bananas states, hatred is now a major ingredient of their relationship. There are surely the vestiges of love—Bananas' belief in Artie's talent and her jealousy of Bunny; Artie's guilt and intermittent tenderness—but her sickness, their drab life, and Artie's restlessness over his unfulfilled dream have set them apart, and Artie has sought solace with Bunny Flingus.

The actual extent of Artie's ambivalence toward his wife is projected in two separate incidents. In one of these, Artie recounts to Bananas his dream about Ronnie as the Pope. He tells how Pope Ronald invited him into a sparkling limousine, but rejected Bananas. Pope Ronald then took him to the cathedral, put him in charge of writing all the church hymns, and made him a saint of the church. Cruelly, he caps off his story with "You weren't invited, Bananas. Ronnie loved only me" (p. 26).

Later, in Act I, however, after Bananas poetically recounts her destroyed life and the etiology of her illness, Artie shows much concern for her welfare. Bananas' symbolic verbal collage relates a dream incident in which she aided four celebrities by offering them a ride in the Shaughnessy automobile, "the green latrine"; the ride ends in four flat tires and in Bananas' abandonment by the celebrities. Later that night she had seen a bruised Bob Hope, one of her passengers, telling jokes about her on the Johnny Carson Show. She is proud to be the center of the jokes, even anonymously, but is sad that the people do not love her, especially since she understands them so well. Through this story's view of her frustrated life, Bananas speaks to us of the lives of so many people in America, and the sense that our culture does nothing but put up barriers among people, making love and communication impossible. By teasing us with the fabled union of fame and happiness, our culture lures people to pursue dazzling dreams frantically; the emptiness of the dream and the failure to realize "success" leave people like Bananas and Artie mad and/or entirely crushed.

When Artie hears her story of the four celebrities, he excitedly and lovingly urges her to seek a cure for her sickness by going to the Pope. She runs to the television set and tries to kiss the image of the Pope's garment, but all she finds is a cold screen. This symbolizes the gaudy lure yet quintessential loneliness imposed by American culture. Artie himself then pushes Bananas aside and hugs the television screen, begging the Pope to help him. These symbols of religion and "culture" are Artie's last chances for salvation. Between Artie and Bananas, two pitiful people, the embers of love, hope, and caring remain, but they have been almost entirely smothered in pain.

Artie met Bunny Flingus, as he tells Billy by phone, when he mistakenly wandered into the women's section of a Turkish bath and "kind of raped her." Sex continues between them, but as Bunny freely admits, she's "a bad lay"; as her name indicates, there are many who have found this out for themselves. She tries to lure him into marriage with promises of gourmet cooking and will not cook for him until after the wedding. Here, Guare is mocking an American courtship ritual; also, through the food passion, he comments on a lack of spirituality in human relationships.

What Bunny does for Artie is to reactivate his hopes. Although Bunny is shallow, ignorant, capable of cruelty and selfishness (as with Bananas), materialistic, and self-centered, she tells Artie that his songs are wonderful. If he would push a little, and use his friend Billy, he would be rich and famous. Artie believes her and calls Billy. Here Guare comments on the materialistic foundation of much of what we call friendship in America. While Billy seems much more interested in hearing about Bananas (to whom he was once apparently attracted) and talking about the recent death of Georgina, the conversation ends with Artie and Bunny jubilantly anticipating a trip to California.

The onomastic device (Bananas, a wife who has gone insane; Bunny Flingus, suggesting sex and transience; Billy Einhorn, the first name suggesting adolescence and the second the lucky break as well as incipient diabolism) helps to create a ridiculous, wild, and yet satiric atmosphere. The names, like the exaggerated behavior of Bananas, the passion of Artie for food, the à la mode dress of the overweight Bunny, the wild dreams and monologues, and Ronnie's behavior, all take this play out of the realm of normal events. However, all these devices still allow a meaningful projection of strains within American culture; the farcical extremes allow a satiric message that could not have been presented in purely naturalistic drama. The moments of tenderness between Artie and Bananas and the quasi-poetic treatment of the tree of blue leaves indicate that the zany, extreme social world of tawdry American commercialism and cultural isolation are not Guare's only target. He is also attuned to the alienated, humiliating condition of man and woman on this earth.

Act II, which is divided into two scenes, is more zany than Act I, and Guare's antireligious fervor comes through in this act with new, vivid ferocity. The act begins with Ronnie standing in the same position as at the end of Act I. He continues to stare at the audience, then makes a time bomb by wiring two grenades to his father's alarm clock. Appearing at once innocent and diabolical, Ronnie delivers a monologue about how his father and everyone else disparage him. He also speaks of his first meeting with Billy Einhorn, and how his failure to attract Billy when Billy was searching for a child to play Huck Finn initially brought on his father's derogation. He warns us that, after tonight, no one will laugh at him again:

* * *

By tonight, I'll be on headlines all over the world.

* * *

I'll show you all. I'll be too big for any of you (p. 63).

After his monologue, a kind of second-act prologue, Ronnie returns to his room with the time bomb.

Artie enters and expresses a wish that Bunny and Bananas could get along and that they could all live together as a happy family. He does not have long to dwell on this thought; it is cut off by the entrance of Corrinna Stroller, a beautiful and famous movie star, Billy Einhorn's fiancée. Corrinna explains to the audience that she was injured in a movie she made with Billy, and is stone deaf, dependent on a transistorized hearing aid. She disconnects her transistors because of a feedback problem. Artie and Bunny worship her as the epitome of Hollywood glamor; unaware of her deafness, they insist on serenading her with Artie's songs. Artie proceeds with the "audition" (Bunny's term) until he is interrupted by three shivering nuns at the back window grate. They have been accidentally locked on the roof while waiting to see the Pope. They look more like monkeys than nuns and, although Bunny tries to keep them out, Artie is touched by their plight and lets them in to watch the Pope on television. Startled by the appearance of the nuns at the window, Corrinna drops her transistors and cannot find them.

It is in his treatment of the nuns that Guare presents his most acrid satire and achieves his most hilarious moments. The group includes an authoritarian head nun, a middle-sized nun, and a little nun. We learn that they stole the binoculars they were using at the Pope's procession and lost them when they flew out of the second nun's hands "like a miracle in reverse" (p. 72). The nuns love imported beer and peanut butter and are disappointed when they discover that the television is not a color model.

When Bunny tries to excuse herself to Corrinna, who cannot hear her now anyway, Bananas enters. She mistakes the nuns for penguins and assumes that Artie has brought work home from the office. While Corrinna continues to misunderstand and to utter non sequiturs, the nuns reveal their ecstasy over meeting a real movie star. Guare blends his satires of American culture and religion by having the Little Nun gush to Corrinna, "I saw *The Sound of Music* thirty-one times. It changed my entire life" (p. 74). We cannot help but wonder if that American musical comedy actually inspired the nun to take her vows.

Artie shoos the nuns into Ronnie's room; they emerge later and declare that an altar boy is in the bedroom. Bananas recalls that Ronnie was an altar boy when he was young and tells everyone, "He kept us in good with God" (p. 75). Artie, obviously regurgitating a lie from Ronnie, declares that his son has been chosen out of all the soldiers at Fort Dix to be the Pope's altar boy at Yankee Stadium. Soon, Artie continues his "audition," although Corrinna can now hear nothing at all; this is a powerful image of worthless effort and empty dreams.

At Bananas' request, he plays the first song he ever wrote, "I Love You So I Keep Dreaming," and then "White Christmas." He discovers (for the first time) that both songs have the same tune, that he has merely plagiarized Irving Berlin. This indicates how little talent Artie actually has, and he becomes extremely angry at Bananas, slamming her fingers under the piano's fallboard. He believes that she was just trying to embarrass him and he becomes so incensed that, egged on by Bunny, he calls the hospital and arranges to have them pick up Bananas immediately. Bananas frantically begs Corrinna to save her, since Billy Einhorn was always a dear friend. In her terror, Bananas swallows Corrinna's transistors, believing they are her tranquilizers. This makes Corrinna nearly go bananas herself.

Now that Artie has arranged for Bananas to be committed, Bunny, who tritely states that she has always been treated "like an old shoe," becomes ecstatic at the prospect of leaving with Artie for their new life of fame and fortune in California. Both Artie's and Bunny's spirits are dampened, however, when Corrinna asks the nuns to pray for her on her trip to Australia, where she and Billy will marry and remain for two years because she needs an ear operation that is obtainable only in Australia. Meanwhile, Billy plans to make a movie entitled *Kangaroo*. Guare's use of such unimaginative titles as *Warmonger* and *Kangaroo* imply much about Billy's gift to Hollywood "culture."

As the nuns pray for Corrinna, Ronnie enters carrying the time bomb, now gift-wrapped. He tells Artie,

> Pop, I'm going to blow up the Pope and when *Time* interviews me tonight, I won't even mention you. I'll say I was an orphan (p. 84).

Artie is too preoccupied to hear Ronnie's plans. When Corrinna declares she has two tickets to the Pope's Yankee Stadium Mass, the nuns and Ronnie scramble for them. An MP enters to take Ronnie, who is AWOL, back to Fort Dix. The nuns chase Ronnie into his room and the MP follows. Soon the Little Nun emerges from Ronnie's room with the tickets, chased by Ronnie, the two other nuns, and the MP. When Ronnie jumps on the Little Nun, the MP catches and arrests him. The Head Nun grabs the tickets, ordering the Little Nun back to Ridgewood, New Jersey. Ronnie tosses the gift-wrapped bomb to Corrinna, telling her that it is a present for Billy. With that, Corrinna and the two ticketed nuns leave.

The zany physical action continues as the MP struggles with Ronnie and then with Artie. Doctors enter for Bananas; by mistake they straight-jacket Bunny and drag her out. As Artie lunges toward the door to save her, Ronnie pulls him back. There is a terrific explosion. Bunny reenters through the smoke, and Artie runs out to look for Corrinna and the two nuns. Meanwhile, Ronnie, the MP, and the Little Nun continue their struggle. Bananas begins to clean her messy apartment with an unattached vacuum cleaner hose, declaring to the audience that she is good at least for cleaning (obviously untrue). This final tableau of scene one is a wonderful mélange of slapstick, social

criticism, ferocious attacks on religion and religious hypocrisy, and a
further elucidation of the hopeless dreams on which the Shaughnessy
household is built.

Before the curtain rises for scene two, we hear the Pope's broad-
cast from Yankee Stadium, praising all Americans as "a people basing
its conception of life on spiritual values, on a religious sense, on
freedom, on loyalty, on work, on the respect of duty, on family affection, on generosity and courage. . . . "(p. 89). We have seen at least
one character in the play destroy each of these values, one by one.
Guare juxtaposes the Pope's enumeration of the values with the opening tableau of Artie and Billy Einhorn sitting in Artie's living room
watching the Pope on television. Billy is sobbing over Corrinna's
violent death. Artie turns to the audience and introduces us to Billy,
"the one. The only" (p. 90). When Billy sobs that he may give up his
career, Artie urges him to go on, to continue because he brings such
joy to so many people. These words sound sincere, but Artie's deeper
motivation is obvious: he suggests that Billy's next picture should be a
musical, and emphasizes this with a few bars of "Back Together
Again" on the piano. He claims that his life is a failure, held together
only by the laughter Billy brings and the majesty of Billy's life. Here
Guare shows the complexity of Artie. As a pitiful failure who holds
Billy (hero/producer of such blockbuster epics as *Warmonger*) in awe,
Artie does inspire our sympathy. Yet he remains foolish in his awe and
selfish in his manipulations. Billy is an empty hero, and Guare seems to
see the Pope in the same light. Regardless, Artie will keep trying to
use both heroes; he will exact a useful blessing from each if he possibly
can.

When Bananas appears, hoping to make Billy happy, he is made
only sadder. Here the suggestion is again made that Billy was once attracted to Bananas, or that Bananas represents the saner, more
"regular" past that Billy enjoyed before stardom and the death of his
wife. Bananas resents Billy's having given her that nickname. Billy's
sensitivity toward Bananas is evident in his explanation of the
nickname's derivation ("A little Italian girl. What else was I going to
call her?"—p. 94). He is protecting her feelings; it is obvious to
everyone that the nickname is appropriate for far different reasons.

At that moment, the Little Nun reveals that there is a flood, caused
by Bananas' trying to burn Bunny by making hot water from the

shower flood the downstairs. As Artie tries to stem the flood, the Little
Nun expresses admiration for Billy, and Bananas begs Billy to save her
from the insane asylum and to save Ronnie from prison. Just as Artie
had phoned Billy in order to use him, Billy now calls a friend who is a
general to have him get Ronnie out of the brig and out of Vietnam service. Through use of the telephone in both instances, Guare links the
two events to emphasize the hollowness and exploitation that often
pass for friendship in our society. In this latter instance, he also attacks
the illicit use of power and influence in our nation. The Little Nun and
Billy declare their friendship, which they base on the common deaths
of separate friends. Guare is suggesting that in America friendship is
grounded on selfish pursuit (Billy's use of the general, Artie's use of
Billy) or circumstance (death of nuns and Corrinna) rather than on
shared beliefs or emotional communion.

Bunny enters, telling of the flood in her apartment. Billy succumbs
to Bunny's food invitation, forsakes Artie, forgets Corrinna, and asks
Bunny to fly off with him. With her eye always on the main chance,
Bunny readily decides to leave Artie. Artie tries to keep Billy interested in his songs, but Billy has eyes only for Bunny. Billy tells Artie
that he creates only for him and Bananas and needs them as an ideal
audience in order to continue his artistic life. This comment echoes
Artie's earlier statement of dependence. Although Billy is mainly an in-
sincere manipulator and Artie is a stunned, naive, and helpless
dreamer and idealist, both men seem to look pathetically to each other
for support. Billy pays the Little Nun to stay and take care of Bananas,
offering her Bunny's apartment as part of the deal. The Little Nun
readily rejects her calling. She kisses the television set, calling it a
shrine, and declares to the audience,

> Ask and you shall receive. . . . I wanted to be a Bride of Christ but I guess now
> I'm a young divorcee (p. 109).

In this glib speech that combines both scripture and soap opera
stereotyping ("young divorcee"), Guare's nun delivers an explosion of
social commentary on pop culture and short-circuited ideals.

Billy tells Artie to keep Bananas home and to love her. Artie is
once more stuck with his chaotic, nagging reality; he even receives an
urgent call from the zoo, telling him that all his animals are giving
birth.

Although Artie views the departure of Billy and Bunny as the end of his chances to escape this reality, Bananas sees it as her own big chance for a new beginning. She actually becomes beautiful in her ecstasy. In her joy and beauty, Bananas forgives Billy for Bunny, promises to be a better wife, adopts Bunny's promise of good cooking, and starts singing "Back Together Again," interspersed with barking. Artie, seeing her happy, grips her neck and slowly squeezes until she is dead. By thus killing her during her momentary ecstasy, he gives her the only real possibility for joy that exists between them; he also achieves his own escape. Blue leaves begin to fall, indicating his madness. Again, he sings for the audience, but it is a new Artie—confident and happy. This time he has the blue spotlight, and we are struck by the similarity to the blue leaves of the hospital. He is now ready to perform; in his madness, he can perhaps recreate the life of illusion that has just been crudely destroyed by reality.

In *The House of Blue Leaves*, John Guare has used the farcical chaos of the Shaughnessy family to cast a sharp light on American culture and on the dislocated state of human beings. Artie Shaughnessy lives in a world of dreams, lured to them by a materialistic, hero-worshipping American ethos. To Guare, this ethos preys especially on the little people, those who cannot escape economic woes and are taught to revere surface glory rather than to develop inner substance. The gloss of a celebrity's success—beauty, fame, money, glory—becomes the base of the culturally engendered value structure of such people, whose real lives hold defeating pressures. Fantasy persists to make reality dimmer. The nuns crowd around the television set for a glimpse of Jacqueline Kennedy. Guare's use of such understated gesture to show awe of the famous perfectly balances the slapstick chaos of the characters' reality. Moreover, Guare shows, in the Sandra Dee-Annette Funicello reference, that real human suffering is not generally understood in America and furnishes no basis for kindness or shared experience (pp. 36–37). Friendship is hollow; marriage is hollow; affairs are empty; even sex is ultimately unsatisfying where no communion of the spirit exists.

To project his vision, Guare employs names that reveal character or life condition (i.e., onomastic play), slapstick comedy, irreverent imagery, and a powerful juxtapositon of the ridiculous with the painful and pitiful. In his juxtaposition, he often achieves a true poetry of statement and feeling. In so doing, he cuts deeper than the level of social criticism with which his farce, satire, and black comedy are primarily concerned. He literally touches the ineffable loneliness, doomed frustration, and ultimate failure of his characters, and, thus, of all human beings.

Entwining of the Strands

Unlike David Rabe's *Sticks and Bones,* with its savage anger, mundane comedy, and high seriousness of tone, John Guare's *The House of Blue Leaves* is, on the surface, whimsically farcical. Yet the plays are more similar than their divergent tones suggest. Both are concerned with the self-image of a male loser (Ozzie/Artie), both involve the Vietnam war, both reflect their authors' profound dissatisfaction with the superficiality and hollowness of American culture, both are highly experimental in dramatic technique (both, for example, employ a prologue and epilogue, contrary to current dramatic practice), and both relate the emptiness of the American dream to the more frightening notion that the human being is, by nature, a lost and lonely creature. Like Rabe, Guare blends a realistic framework and emotional context with such Absurdist elements as serio-comic action, dark philosophy, and nightmarish atmosphere.

Like *Sticks and Bones, The House of Blue Leaves* possesses a linear plot, albeit a skeletal one. Linear plot, a fundamental characteristic of realistic theatre is, in this play, concerned with the dream of a middle-aged zookeeper to liberate himself from his shabby, painful life by achieving success as a Hollywood songwriter. The pain in his life is based in emotional alienation from his son, the burden of a mentally ill wife, his awareness of his advancing age ("I'm too old to be a young talent!"—p. 109), and his inability to succeed in the few awkward ventures he does make, such as the El Dorado talent show. Dissatisfied at home, Artie, like many American middle-aged men, casually forms a liaison with another woman. This woman, Bunny Flingus, whose life is also shabby, encourages Artie to exploit an old friendship in order to get the big chance they both need so desperately. The old friend, Billy Einhorn, ultimately does not give Artie the break he longs for, but instead runs off with Bunny, in a course of events she enthusiastically accepts. Thus, in his quest for *unattainable* escape, Artie loses Bunny, who represents *attainable* escape. He is left in his real and symbolic zoo, with a leopardess that eats her young and a wife who barks like a dog. Disillusioned by elusive dreams, Artie simply cannot bear to return to a chaotic and shabby reality; therefore, he goes mad, killing his deranged wife in an act of mercy, love, personal liberation, and despair.

The essential realism of plot line, setting, and character exposition is further enhanced by the realistic details of Artie's environment. It is 1965. Artie lives in Queens; his son is AWOL from Fort Dix, where he is scheduled to go to Vietnam; the nuns who invade Artie's apartment are from Ridgewood, New Jersey; and the Pope comes to Yankee Stadium, where he makes an important speech on international affairs and the spiritual well-being of America.

This important detail of the Pope's arrival in New York is certainly realistically grounded, but inasmuch as the Pope represents the possibility of dream fulfillment for millions of people (including Bunny, Artie, and Bananas), the Pope himself and his coming function multidimensionally to mesh the play's realistic substructure and the concomitant Absurdist orientation.

Early in the play, Bunny encourages Artie to leave his apartment, songs in hand, and to wave them before the Pope so that the songs, blessed by the Pope, will achieve success. She also hopes that the Pope will bless their union as a couple, insuring that their committing Bananas and running off will be acceptable behavior. Similarly, Artie encourages Bananas to kiss the image of the Pope on their television screen in the hope that contact with the Pope will result in her recovery. The nuns' literal assault of Ronnie over Corrinna Stroller's tickets to Yankee Stadium mirrors the behavior of Bunny and Artie. If the nuns can somehow be in the presence of the Pope, wonderful things will occur.

The Pope's appearance before a mass audience is, in the mind of Bunny particularly, an incredibly theatrical experience. It is grand showmanship by the world's ultimate celebrity. The Pope on television at Yankee Stadium is the movie star par excellence. This linkage of the Pope with movie stardom works conversely as well. To Artie, Bunny, and Bananas, and apparently to masses of people, the movie star inhabits the empyrean, a special place of infinite possibility. Clearly they believe that if only they can enter this dream world, their problems and pain will pass mysteriously away, and they will live like gods, unaffected by the ravages of time and fate. Guare skillfully emphasizes the foolishness of this dream by making Corrinna Stroller, the character who *appears* to have made it in the dream world, stone deaf.

Despite dreams and the possible chance through Billy Einhorn, Artie fails to reach Nirvana. Bunny, who has clung to Artie as a way to escape, is offered a surer thing, and grabs it. Her departure with Billy, and Billy's selfish rationalization of why Artie must remain in Queens as Billy's "audience," represent the pathetic climax of Artie's quest through hollowness, superficiality, and self-deception. Indeed, the motif of self-deception; of psychological, social, and existential myopia; of prospects unfulfilled; and of dreams turned to dirt is the principal conceptual motif of the play. Again and again, the characters, major and minor, hope and dream, only to experience the blasting apart of their elusive and illusive imaginings. Ronnie tells us in a monologue how he dreamed of being Einhorn's Huck Finn, only to fail and earn his father's ridicule when Billy regards him as a retarded child instead of a prospect for the part. Bananas dreams of attracting dignitaries to her Buick on a rainy day, only to become ineffectual when its tires go flat. Corrinna Stroller hopes to keep her glamorous image intact by hiding her deafness, but becomes totally ridiculous when Bananas swallows her transistors. Later, she reveals her hope to go to Australia for an ear operation, but she is killed. For Artie, the shattered dream experience is his major life pattern and the central movement of Guare's entire drama. Artie enters a talent show at the El Dorado, but no one pays attention and he must purchase his own beers. He dreams that his son as Pope Ronald bestows on him fame—as both songwriter and saint. In reality, Ronnie regards his father with a terrible and superficially hate-filled ambivalence. He is busy with his own perverse plans for fame, as the person who assassinated the Pope. Bunny and Artie hold up his songs before the Pope, but Billy has no time or interest in them; Artie has pictures of movie celebrities tacked up on his living-room wall, but he himself never becomes famous. Rather, he receives word that the zoo animals are giving birth and he is forced into the symbolic role of zookeeper once more. In a poignant moment, Artie kills Bananas in the midst of her happiness because his dreams are destroyed; because her dreams of love and fulfillment are unrealistic; and because he has learned not only that the American dream of success is hollow, but that the vision of a life of fulfillment is a deception. Better madness and the House of Blue Leaves, better death for Bananas and death in life for himself than a reactivation of memories and dreams doomed from the start.

While the play's ironic movement is steady, only at the conclusion—as is characteristic of Absurdist drama—is the dark curtain finally and ineluctably drawn down over the stage of Artie Shaughnessy's life. Until the departure of Billy, a zany, whimsical, farcical quality colors the play and dilutes and postpones, almost entirely obscures, the dark undercurrent of the work. Characteristically, all so-called Absurdist comedy is actually Absurdist tragedy with a comic veneer; Beckett's *Waiting for Godot*, a prototype of the genre, has a comic surface overlying a dark substratum. This is an essential technique of Absurdist drama and a tenet of its life philosophy as well. In *The House of Blue Leaves*, the zany surface provides a vehicle for Guare's social irreverence; simultaneously, it fulfills the conventional Absurdist modal dichotomy. Artie's silly songs; the onomastic play in the names Bunny Flingus, Bananas, Corrinna Stroller, and Billy Einhorn; Ronnie's bomb episode; the appearance of three monkeylike nuns at Artie's window and their subsequent slapstick and irreverent interactions; Bunny's naively ridiculous dialogue, and her practice of winning men with food instead of sex; Bananas' clothing, irrationality, cooking of Brillo, and swallowing of Corrinna's transistors; the entire scene in which Artie and Bunny court Corrinna's attentions while she cannot hear a word they are saying—each of these facets of the play is comic, and together they provide a potentially hilarious atmosphere.

The hilarity is muted, however, for we realize from the moment the play begins that Guare is employing comic techniques to attack obliquely the materialism, religious hypocrisy, brutality, and gaudiness of American culture; he knows that direct, serious frontal attack would be heavy-handed and uselessly offensive. Similarly, the comic surface is a suspenseful plotting technique and provides a needed contrast to the terribly touching and terribly frightening depiction of the human condition. As with *Sticks and Bones*, Guare's play manages to convey a deeply felt antipathy to the American ethos. As with *Sticks and Bones*, a realistic skeleton—believable family, environment, and qualities of

character and plot—are richly interwined with the serio-comic techniques and dark vision of the Absurdist theatre.

Notes

[1]Henry Hewes, "The Playwright as Voyager," *Saturday Review*, 20 November 1973,
p. 48.

[2]Patricia Bosworth, "Yes for a Young Man's Fantasies," *The New York Times*, 7
March 1971, II, p. 12.

[3]Harold Clurman, "Theatre," *The Nation*, 1 March 1971, p. 285.

[4]Julius Novick, "Very Funny—Or a Long Sick Joke?," *The New York Times*, 21
February 1971, II, p. 9.

[5]Edith Oliver, "Off Broadway," *The New Yorker*, 20 February 1971, p. 90.

[6]Henry Hewes, "Under the Rainbow," *Saturday Review*, 20 March 1971, p. 10.

[7]Clurman, p. 285.

[8]Bosworth, p. 12.

[9]Clive Barnes, "Theater: John Guare's *House of Blue Leaves* Opens," *The New York
Times*, 11 February 1971, p. 54.

[10]Bosworth, p. 12.

[11]Novick, p. 9.

[12]Bosworth, p. 12.

[13]Novick, p. 9.

[14]Clurman, p. 285.

[15]Barnes, p. 54.

[16]Walter Kerr, "The Most Striking New American Play," *The New York Times*, 4
April 1971, II, p. 3.

[17]Hewes, "Rainbow," p. 10.

[18]Oliver, p. 90.

[19]Kerr, p. 3.

[20]Oliver, p. 90.

[21]Hewes, "Rainbow," p. 10.

[22]Kerr, p. 3.

[23]Hewes, "Voyager," p. 48.

[24]*Ibid.*

[25]*Ibid.*

[26]John Guare, "Foreword," *The House of Blue Leaves* (New York: Viking Press,
1972), pp. vii–xiii. All pages cited are from this edition.

The Taking of Miss Janie

ED BULLINS

IV

A Review of the Criticism

The Taking of Miss Janie was produced in 1975. There is not yet a large body of criticism; that which does exist is essentially limited to newspaper and magazine reviews. Despite this paucity of material, however, clear critical contours have emerged, and most critics regard the work as an original and meaningful contribution to American drama. In *The Nation*, for example, on April 5, 1975, Harold Clurman states that it is "a forcefully telling play." He further states:

> The play, despite its disturbing revelations, is neither mournful in tone nor tendentiously raucous. Vigorously humorous, it does not whine; it growls with a savage grin. Without pleading any special cause, it has sinew and muscle. Bold in its courageous objectivity, it is by no means depressing.[1]

Mel Gussow, writing in *The New York Times*, asserts that the play is "provocative."[2] While such comments are typical of the overall positive reaction to the play, Barbara Mackay and especially Stanley Kauffmann are quite critical. Mackay claims that the play is politically retrograde,[3] and Kauffmann attacks both the thought and the structure: ". . . all we are getting is examples, not drama, [and] Bullins has absolutely no *ideas* on his subject, he can only present bits of it as evidence."[4]

Unlike Kauffmann, most critics find the play's structure appropriate, even attractive. All agree that the play opens and closes with the rape of a white woman by a black man, and that the body of the work, set for the most part at a party, Bullins' favorite setting, provides glimpses of the lives of young blacks and whites of the sixties. Even Kauffmann concurs that "Bullins wants to examine the texture and movement of the sixties at a focal point of the decade's dynamics:

socially and politically radical college students."[5] Edith Oliver, in an article entitled "Fugue for Three Roommates," most eloquently epitomizes critical reaction to the play's structure. She refers to the opening and closing scenes as "prologue" and "epilogue," and states that the play "can be most briefly described as a fugue, whose themes are the feelings and experiences of a number of young people during the nineteen-sixties." Since the play is characterized by intermittent monologues, Oliver compares it technically to *The Fabulous Miss Marie*, also by Bullins. As in that play, "each of the leading characters, with a spotlight on him, talks at one time or another directly to the audience about what is on his mind and in his heart and, occasionally, what lies in store for him." Finally, Oliver calls the play "clear" and "complex."[6]

Mel Gussow of *The New York Times* also comments on the complexity of its structure, comparing it favorably with Bullins' earlier work *The Pig Pen*, to which *The Taking of Miss Janie* is a sequel. Praising the structure, Gussow says: "The play moves in and out of the party, forward and backward until we have a complete picture of a society in limbo."[7] Similarly laudatory, Clive Barnes asserts in *The New York Times* that "the quick dissolving scenes . . . offer the image of a period seen through the distorting glass of a special mind."[8] Walter Kerr, however, in a third *New York Times* review, states:

> The play's frame doesn't really contain or explain the things that shimmer inside it, and quite apart from our losing the two principals for long stretches of time, we are left wondering why Janie's "taking" should be made to serve as summary of a decade's mishaps and misapprehensions.

Kerr contends that the structure is confusing and the play unclear, stating:

> No one likes having to finish—or trying to finish—an author's play for him; but that's the effort asked here, and you'll have to put yourself through it if you want to take something home from [the play].[9]

Kerr, however, does find a clearly statable theme: "The 60's, we gradually learn if we pay extremely close attention, were years of self-delusion."[10] Kerr's negative judgment on the overall relation of structure to conception is similar to that of Clive Barnes. Barnes argues that "the play could do with a sharper focus. . . . [i]t is a failure of total clarification on the part of the playwright—but the man can write like an angel."[11] Less negative than Kerr, Barnes goes on to claim that the play's construction is "unusual, yet also highly effective."[12]

In their ambivalence toward matters of structure and clarity, Barnes and Kerr are echoed by other critics, who see basic flaws in other works by Bullins. In *America* (May 31, 1975), Catharine Hughes expresses this widely held attitude:

> He is certainly not the best writer, for he is not at all good in constructing a play. His works ramble, are diffuse, at times seem almost a catch-as-catch-can of black life in America. And there, in a sense, lies his effectiveness: Bullins play is alive. Few others are.[13]

Although Hughes goes on to claim that Bullins seems unwilling to construct a play carefully, although she considers *Miss Janie* to lack economy, depth, and nuance, she is quite affirmative in her overall view of the play: "It could be a better play, but it reflects a great deal of where we are, and, more particulary, why."[14]

This tendency to criticize the play's construction or opacity and yet find the work significant, meaningful, and appealing is typical of most of the criticism. Aligning himself with Barnes and Kerr, Mel Gussow states: "Approaching allegory, Mr. Bullins is trading in stereotypes, but he never loses sight of the truth that informs the cliché."[15] Charles Young, a free-lance writer who interviewed Bullins, calls the play "a brutal satire of abandoned ideals and the revolution that never was."[16] He claims that during a succession of scenes, we watch the characters grow old in America. He elicits from Bullins the statement that the theme of the play is "the destruction of illusion."[17] T. E. Kalem contends in *Time* that the rape "is less a brutal physical act than the saddest of requiems." The play itself is a "double requiem," for both the "anarchic violence" and "the defeated hopes of the '60's." Kalem goes on to praise the vivid street idiom, the structure, and the seductive atmosphere of the play. He says that the production "is an auspicious beginning for Joseph Papp's plan to bring fresh plays into Lincoln Center's Newhouse Theater, some by black and Hispanic playwrights."[18]

Only Kauffmann is unyielding on the notions of both clarity and quality. He admits that the work is theatrically attractive, which, according to the Bullins interview with Charles Young, is one of Bullins' primary goals. Kauffmann also agrees that "the framework—the fated 'rape'—is good." However, he claims that Bullins "never decided, in artistic terms, why he wanted to write [the play] and what he was going to do about it." Like other Bullins' plays, this one is "ragged and raging; raging but ragged; a strong personal voice that often lapses into clichés of dialogue and construction." Moreover, while Bullins' street idiom is effective, Kauffmann claims, his straight conversation is not realistic and neither Flossy nor Peggy is an effective character. What Kauffmann is saying, in essence, is that despite an exciting conception, the play lacks artistic substance and coherence; to use Kauffmann's word, it lacks "depth."[19]

The matter of depth, of course, is related to both theme and clarity—to what the work is trying to say and how clearly it makes its statement. Critics either differ on these matters, or they dodge them by omission or vagueness. For example, Barbara Mackay contends that Bullins elevates rape "into an act of supreme liberation from white oppression." She finds this symbolism depressing, saying it rests on an assumption of black inferiority.[20] As mentioned, Kalem sees the rape as "an image of the anarchic violence of the '60's."[21] Clive Barnes believes the play to be a black overview of the sixties, concerned primarily with black mistrust of whites. According to Barnes, Bullins' attitude is expressed by Monty in the simple question, "How is a white broad going to dig 'Down with Whitey' poems?"[22] Kerr, by contrast, can draw no conclusion about the rape:

> Is physical conquest the only answer to the thousand questions raised; was "rape" the resolution the sixties ought to have been seeking? Or is Janie no more than a nitwit, making impossibly childish demands in a situation too grave for children? The play's structure doesn't say.[23]

Some critical replies to the charges of emptiness and confusion are furnished by those critics who concur with Bullins' claim that it is not a message play. As Bullins states to Charles Young:

> I don't write to please the audience and reassure everyone that we agree. I don't care how they feel or what they think—whether they agree or disagree—just so it makes them examine themselves. In a work like this, the truth is open-ended. Like Hemingway said, "If I wanted to send a message, I'd go to Western Union."[24]

Clive Barnes affirms this view:

> Although Mr. Bullins is clearly a moral writer, he never moralizes. His point of view is not so much argued out on stage, but presented as a documentary, and documented truth.[25]

Even more stimulating is the suggestion of Harold Clurman:

> The audience laughs, shouts, and stamps in recognition of the types and situations depicted. It is itself the material of what it beholds and is puzzled on that

account. It, too, does not *know*. It finds it impossible "to take sides" and it constantly veers in its sympathies because Bullins does not seek to direct it to any firm conclusion. He is demonstrating, not preaching. His voice here, for all its explosive resonance, is essentially poetic.[26]

A Discussion

In 1975, *The Taking Of Miss Janie* won the Obie Award and the New York Drama Critics' Circle Award as the best play of the 1974–1975 season. A sequel to *The Pig Pen*, which portrayed events at a party held on the night of the assassination of Malcolm X, *Miss Janie* is one of a series of Bullins' plays dealing with the black experience in America. Beginning in 1968 with an evening of one-act plays presented off Broadway, Bullins has provided a steady stream of one-acters and full-length works. In 1971, he won an Obie Award for *In New England Winter*. Winner of the Vernon Rice Award and recipient of fellowships from the Rockefeller and Guggenheim Foundations, Bullins is a prodigious producer and one of the significant new voices in American theatre.

The Taking of Miss Janie, which is a long one-act play, is concerned with black/white relations in America. As its title suggests, the play focuses upon the rape of a white woman by a black man. Actually, it is a second sexual assault that is imminent when the play begins; Janie (or "Miss Janie," to use Monty's disparaging nickname, a throwback to slave/owner relationships) has already been raped by Monty once. In the prologue, which is angry and bitter in tone, Monty stalks Janie. As we move into the body of the play, a flashback, we wonder whether this second sexual attack will actually take place. When we return to the rape sequence in the epilogue, the tone is of sadness and resignation in Janie and of increasing anger in Monty. Ironically, instead of showing us the completion of the second assault, the epilogue takes us to a time that is immediately prior to the first encounter. Moreover, the epilogue seems to happen both in the present (like the prologue) and in the past. This purposeful ambiguity of both time and process reflects the tone of the entire play.

Neither the extemely theatrical and sensational rape, nor even the sexual relationship of Janie and Monty per se, is of deepest concern to Bullins. Rather, Bullins uses the relationship of the couple and their relationships with the other seven characters essentially as a means for exploring black/white relations in America. It is the vividness, the power, the violence, and the social and psychological insight that makes Bullins' exploration compelling; all of these elements are then meshed with theatrical experimentalism, making the play new and excitingly different.

Structurally, the work is divided into twelve sections; each section is then further subdivided.

Although the entire work is exposition, the *first section*, beginning with Janie's monologue, introduces us to the present situation of the two principal characters, Monty and Janie. Janie, who has just been raped by Monty, sits tearfully at the end of his bed, trying to communicate with him. She is trying to understand why Monty, who has been a close friend, would wish to mistreat her and destroy their friendship. Monty simply stalks her, calls her "bitch," and says that she knew from the start that their relationship would come to this. Janie denies this, and the point is left moot in the play itself; she claims that all she ever wanted was their friendship. Apparently, Monty is unimpressed by her denial and her entreaty to him to desist.

Section two, introduced by a slide of Monty and Janie dressed in the styles of the late fifties, is a flashback. We watch as they meet, fellow students in a creative writing class. After class, Janie expresses admiration for Monty's writing; although its bitterness repels her, she recognizes Monty's talent and sensitivity. When she asks him, "Do you call that Black Poetry?" (p. 4),[27] she exhibits a naiveté that will continue to characterize her, in some measure, throughout the play. But Janie is not simply "naive"; she is a symbolically complex character; paradoxically, her portrayal, like that of the other characters, is flawed and only partially realized in the play. Along with the naiveté that enables her to enter the black world and form a friendship with Monty, there is also a shallowness and selfishness in Janie that makes it impossible for her, at least at the outset, to draw really close to Monty. Reacting against the conventional controls of her parents, she dabbles—and essentially trifles—with the lives of people she cannot possibly understand at her stage of development. Wishing to be arty and chic—and longing to partake of the more dynamic, more directed lives of the blacks—she tries desperately to interact and to

belong. But her commitment is incomplete, and she protects herself
with a degree of aloofness. She is a symbol of the American ethos that
uses blacks but never totally accepts them; unable to fuse herself to
and identify with Monty, she also represents white liberals who interact socially with blacks but essentially fail to understand or respond
to them. Although Bullins' conscious intention may not have been
realized in the play, he has summarized Janie's position in his interview
with Charles Young,

> Janie was very dishonest. She knew what Monty wanted; he never disguised
> his intentions. But she still was trying to keep him as her own little slave or
> eunuch.[28]

The play gives us insufficient opportunity to enter Janie's mind
and to observe her maturation, which does occur; she assents, albeit
sadly, to the rape. Because we do not witness her development, we find
it difficult to accept her as a real human being, and her symbolic dimension is sometimes obscure. For example, her language is often trite and
poetically false. She continually utters lines that are hardly believable
from a fairly intelligent college student. While such triteness might indicate her shallowness, and such poetic falseness might indicate her
desperate attempt to be provocative and deep like Monty and the other
black characters, the lines often are simply too awkward for a realistic
character. In essence, the transition back and forth from realistic
character to symbol is rich and intriguing, but not always clear and
smooth.

During this initial scene in the flashback, Monty coins the "Miss
Janie" nickname. She objects, but he persists, saying that this name
will be a secret between them. His tone is mocking rather than bitter or
angry. He invites Janie to a party at his apartment. She finds the prospect of his poetry reading an enticement to come, but she hopes that
his tone will not be as despairing as it was in class.

The party is the *third* major *section* of the work. Before the guests
arrive, Monty's roommates, Rick and Len, casually argue, exposing us
to their divergent black politics. Rick is essentially a Black Nationalist
who detests whites and attacks Len for interacting with them. His
rhetoric prepares us for his mistreatment of Janie upon her arrival as
the first guest. Rick first slams the door in her face, then tells her her

sin was being born, and finally calls her a "devil lady" (p. 11). Both
Monty and Len, who are more hospitable to whites, try to soften the effect of Rick's attack.

After Janie, a series of other people arrive at the party. First to arrive is Peggy, a sensitive and intelligent black woman; she also
mistreats Janie, and seems to interact best with Rick. Next is Sharon, a
young, middle-class white Jewish woman, who is Len's friend. She arrives at the same time as Lonnie, Janie's jazz-playing boyfriend, who is
the epitome of the shallow person who feels compelled to be "hip." In
Monty's very first monologue, he indicates his displeasure at Janie's
inviting this white boyfriend to a party to which he invited her alone.

Flossy arrives next. She is a hard, sensual black woman of the
streets, who is involved in a casual sexual relationship with Monty. She
has little to say during the party, other than expressing hunger and
thirst. Shortly after Flossy, Mort Silberstein arrives, a mythic figure of
the 1950s beat generation, now out of date but trying to hold on to a
feeling of significance. He has a bad drug habit and no available funds.
He tries to manipulate a loan from Monty, telling him that the price of
drugs has risen. We meet these characters singly as they arrive and
meet each other; this is an extremely smooth technique for introducing
characters.

While much of this party section is a matter of introductions, the
black/white strain is a continual undercurrent. It appears in discussion
(e.g., Lonnie's having learned black music in school) and in certain
symbolic gestures (e.g., Mort Silberstein arrives singing and dancing a
rock hora, and as the individuals watch, they divide into separate racial
camps). The racial issue is kept at the fore, primarily by Rick's acidic
commentaries on the fall of Western civilization, his jibes at the white
guests (he states that he would like to pour gasoline on Janie), his Black
Moslem rhetoric about pork, his repeated slurs on Jews, and his expressed dissatisfaction with his roommates over their friendliness to
the alleged "devil" whites.

This section also repeats the monologue technique and the surrealism of the first section. During the party, both Monty and Janie
present monologues. These monologues are clearly distinguishable
from the somewhat briefer, more aggressive speeches of Rick. Monty
uses his monologue to express anger at Janie for inviting Lonnie, to
assert his own superiority to white males, to argue that Janie is teasing

and stringing him along, and to foreshadow that he will physically dominate her in the end, no matter how long it takes. By contrast, Janie uses her monologue to tell us that she is attracted only platonically to Monty. He is sensitive, serious, and talented, and she hopes that they will form a lasting friendship. As for Lonnie, he is not talented and really means nothing to her. Therefore, she will resist Monty's sexual entreaties not because of Lonnie or because of Monty's blackness—she has "made it with black guys before" (p. 22)—but because she does not want to intensify, complicate, and thus spoil their potential friendship. Idealizing their "black/white love," Janie hopes that their friendship will mature "like sweet grapes change with age and care into a distinctive bouquet upon choice, rare wines" (p. 22). This is bad, trite poetry, surrealistically imposed here and occasionally elsewhere upon Janie's naturalistic dialogue. While Janie's desire for friendship is sincere, her banal language suggests a shallow understanding of what such a friendship would entail.

Examples of other significant surrealistic elements involve the use of light and motion. For example, Mort enters from the shadows, suggesting his ghostlike qualities; he is the spirit of the fifties, when activism was simpler, and his kind of beat liberalism was acceptable to blacks. Now he is only an outdated cliché. The monologues are presented in an isolated lighted spot to emphasize separate states of consciousness. Also, the dancelike motions of the characters and the changes in light take us beyond the atmosphere of this party to a consideration of the larger outside situation—American racial strife in general.

These imaginative elements complement the overall surrealistic rendering of Monty's apartment, which in Bullins' words, is "an abstract depiction of a decade of cheap living spaces" (p. 1). Indeed, it is only a subtle change of lighting that takes us from this party to a meeting, years later, between Janie and Monty.

Section four is concerned with this subsequent meeting between Janie and Monty. Janie does not wish to give birth to Lonnie's baby and asks Monty to help her get an abortion. By now Monty is her special friend, and she comes to him when there is no one else to turn to. He readily agrees to help her so that she will not have to tell her parents, who would be horrified. Monty offers her money and his apartment for recuperation. However, when he offers her love, she withdraws, not wishing to involve them in a way that will harm their friendship. When Monty calls her "Miss Janie," she says they are so close that she no longer even resents that old epithet.

The *fifth section* begins a steady series of monologues that punctuate the play until, in its final section, the play cyclically returns to a conversation between Monty and Janie that, paradoxically, preceded the prologue itself. Each monologue is followed by a dialogue between the monologist and a second character; often, additional related interactions, involving more characters, occur as well. In many of the monologues, time jumps forward to the future. Peggy, whose monologue begins this fifth section, concentrates on her relationship with Monty, whom she married, with whom she had a child, and from whom she is now separated. Peggy speaks in decidedly racist terms about black love, black men, and black women. She tells us that Monty is selfish and cruel and loves only himself. However, she reveals that she still wants Monty, despite the pain she has suffered, particularly in having to give up her child for adoption. She likens Monty to a con man; he married her, fathered her child, sent her to work so that he could go to school, and then left her.

Peggy's story continues in a dialogue with Flossy. She tells Flossy how she married a white boy after Monty left her, almost causing Monty to become a Black Nationalist out of jealousy and rage. She also reveals that she knows of Flossy's sex with Monty behind her back, to which Flossy answers only, "Well, you know that my thing is making it with my friend-girl's ole men, honey" (p. 25).

With the major focus still on Peggy, the scene permits a subdivided flashback illustration of the period of her marriage to Monty. A light comes up on another part of the stage, and a minor episode unfolds. Janie has arrived in San Francisco to visit Monty. Her arrival is interrupted by Flossy's appearance; it is obvious that Monty and Flossy are very deeply involved sexually. Here, Janie again speaks an awkward poetic line that reflects her character, yet weakens the scene:

> I didn't know you had someone besides me . . . somebody real . . . somebody
> black and sensual as the night who would blot out my pale image like a cloud
> covering a dim, far constellation (p. 26).

In the execution of this flashback scene, Flossy has moved over to join Monty and Janie. Returning to Peggy, Flossy recounts Monty's sex with her and poetry reading with Janie. When Flossy calls black men evil, Peggy declares she's a Lesbian, and she and Flossy passionately embrace.

Section six is Lonnie's monologue. He, too, speaks of his past, particularly of his past with Janie. After blaming his contemporaries and himself for feeding parasitically on each other, he speaks of his long and intense relationship with Janie. He speaks of the influence Janie's parents exercise upon her (her never-ending student life is a result) and of Janie's need for independence, which drew them apart. When Janie had three abortions, he began to feel guilty; then she began to feel stifled by him, and they broke up. Although Lonnie now declares he is a member of the Baha'i World Faith, a believer in a world family of all mankind, he reiterates his anti-black prejudices that he spouted earlier at the party, including his characteristic use of the pejorative *spade*.

After his monologue, Lonnie argues with Rick. Rick calls Lonnie a devil and a Jew. Lonnie tells Rick that he has renounced his Judaism and wishes to be characterized as a human being, not a devil. But when Rick persists, Lonnie loses his temper and exits. Rick feels triumphant. With this section as with the last, it is hard to specify the time sequence. Bullins' blurring of time relationships, his detailing of the lives of minor characters (in the initial list of characters, he refers to both major and minor characters as "people"), his use of direct address to the audience, his discussion of large social themes, and the cyclical structure of the play all serve to expand the play's horizons, to reflect powerfully on the American ethos, not simply to depict the particular relationship between Monty, a black man, and Janie, a white woman.

Len, whose monologue begins *section seven*, speaks not so much of past events in his life as of the influence he has had upon others. He speaks of himself as a teacher and explains that he got Monty interested in drama and introduced Rick to Black Nationalism. Like a seer, he foretells the rise and fall of Rick as a Black Nationalist leader, and foresees the assassinations of the Kennedys, Martin Luther King, and Malcolm X. Len says to the audience: "Tonight you are looking into some of the makings of the sixties . . . which, of course, went to make the seventies" (p. 30). Characterizing the play as an "integrated social epic," he explains that Bullins only hinted at matters because he did not know the impacts of the "accidental associations" he depicted. Thus, surrealistically, a character looks at his author as a limited being, limited at least in comparison with himself. Len regards himself as a kind of progenerative seed upon which Bullins had only a limited perspective. "He did not know," Len says, "that through me he would discover the kernel of political truth of the era, the seminal social vision of the sweep of so much history" (p. 30).

From this monologue, Len proceeds to converse with Sharon. This is presumably a conversation in the distant past when Len and Sharon hardly knew each other. He describes himself as a rational intellectual, and she tells him that she does not like his revolutionary friends. She wonders if he considers her a devil, and he assures her he does not. Sharon tells him of her sexual rebellion—that she has slept with over seventy men—and he simply replies that she is a child of the times. He is deeply attracted to her.

Len moves out of the light, and *section eight* begins with Sharon's monologue. Time has passed since Len and Sharon first became involved with each other; she speaks of their marriage and the birth of their son. Essentially, she says that although times were occasionally very rough, she and Len finally worked things out. He continues to think of himself as an intellectual, but has become a middle-class businessman. Sharon is proud that they have stayed together; unlike most black/white couples, they have managed to live harmoniously. Surely, despite Len's loss of radical commitment, their lasting relationship is an optimistic note in the play.

Mort Silberstein is not, however, as enthusiastic about Sharon's marriage as she is, as he expresses in the subsequent dialogue with her. Mort accuses her of adding "racial suicide to cultural injury" by marrying Len (p. 33). This attitude shows him to be a narrow racist, and Sharon proves him to be a hypocrite; she reveals that he is having an affair with a German girl even though superficially he is a confirmed Jewish zealot. Actually, we find he is filled with self-hatred, declaring he could never marry a Jewish girl and expressing deep resentment toward his mother who allegedly drowned him in chicken soup and tried to bury him in bagels and lox. (Bullins is less acute in treating the Jewish ethos than he is in projecting the overall relationship of blacks and whites.) Finally, Mort becomes utterly ridiculous when he explains his attachment to Nina, the German girl, by pointing to the internationalist orientation of her Marxism. He can praise Nina's internationalism but cannot accept Sharon's interracial marriage. Sharon caps the conversation by saying that the only reality for her is her black baby (i.e., in white America) and by declaring that she does not care who killed Jesus (i.e., these narrow, silly religious arguments and prejudices have no place in her mind or in her life).

Section nine emerges with a monologue by Flossy. The setting is a party at Monty's apartment. Once again, the exact time frame is difficult to establish. We do know that we are at a rather early party thrown by Monty. Instead of speaking of herself, Flossy speaks mostly of Monty, with whom she has had sex intermittently, and who treats her like a lady and enjoys her sensuality. She contends that, unlike other male friends, Monty is gaining a clear vision of himself; he is achieving emotional health. His only flaw is chasing after white girls; if he would only let himself, he and Peggy might get together. Flossy sees herself as too unsteady a companion for Monty.

Flossy's monologue shifts to dialogue with Janie. She first expresses hostility toward Janie because Janie is white and because Monty seems so allured by her. Janie, showing aloofness but a sudden hint of new maturity, counters: "Maybe he's got what he wants from you . . . and he wants what he thinks he can get from me" (p. 36). While such a sentiment might suggest that Janie is stringing Monty along, it is simply objective observation by an uninvolved Janie. Flossy seems impressed with Janie's hipness and pulls her aside to teach her to play The Game (i.e., the sex game). Flossy enjoys helping a girl with sexual potential, thus psychologically eliminating Janie, a white woman, as a competitor; but Janie is merely bewildered by Flossy's advice and exhortations.

Section ten begins with a monologue by Rick, presumably at the same party. He reports an old motif: his dissatisfaction with integrated social events. He particularly scorns Len for planning to marry Sharon and Monty for waiting so long for sex from Janie. To Rick, this chasing of white women epitomizes the confusion of the blacks in the sixties; stepping (as Len did earlier) outside time, Rick contends that the confusion will last into the seventies as well. He feels that the black women are also doing strange things, that "This is Babylon" and, as he said earlier, "the beginning of the end" (p. 37). Peggy offers to give him a ride downtown in her new sports car. Rick pompously addresses

Peggy, calling her life unnatural and assessing her troubles partly as
the result of Monty's sexual exploitation, association with white devils,
and other psychosocial factors. Peggy accuses him of distorting the
truth; they did not have parties to impress white girls. Instead, they
were part of the sixties generation that believed in integration. Rick
continues to deride her broken life and to blame Western culture for
making her a freak. Angered now, she counters by mentioning Rick's
future drug problems, his torturing of young black women, and his
political problems as a powerful Cultural Nationalist. To make these
points, Peggy must transcend the present and speak as a seer of the
future. Rick disputes her forecast:

> . . . why don't you keep quiet about all that? It ain't even happened yet. So be
> cool (p. 39).

Rick claims he already knows his future and that it will be "glorious."
Peggy poignantly argues that "we all failed" (p. 39). By "we" she
means the youth of the sixties, a youth with great potential; "We just
turned out lookin' like a bunch of punks and freaks and fuck-offs"
(p. 39). She goes on to tell Rick that he is living in the past. When Rick
no longer wants her ride, she declares that she is going to stay at the
party and have sex with Monty in memory of the relationship she had
with him. She adds: "I can't just let the Miss Janie's dance off with the
world, can I?" (p. 40). Rick encourages her and concludes with the existential line: "Ya know, it be about what you make it anyway" (p. 40).

The *eleventh section* begins with the last of the monologues, that by
Mort Silberstein. Mort, in his hip language, a language captured as
well as the black street idiom by Bullins, claims the world is confused
and ugly, a bad party, "the worst party of the decade. . . . Probably the
worse goddamn party in memory" (p. 40). Despite his social
awareness, Mort is unable to direct or save himself. He is still a beat
poet, after his time, and a confirmed drug addict. At the end of his
monologue, he begs the audience for money to buy a fix.

As Monty enters, Mort says: "Hey, Monty. Tell these folks [the
audience] how bad I need ten bucks" (p. 40). Monty rejects Mort's request and, in fact, rejects Mort entirely. An exchange of charges and a
violent argument ensues. Monty withdraws from Mort's drugs and
ultra-Jewishness, and Mort refers to black people as "spades." When
Mort persists in reviling black politics, Monty hits him and shouts:

I don't want to be a whiteman, do you hear me, Mort Silberstein? I don't want to be a token Jew even. I'm me. You understand? It's taken a long time but I know that now (p. 41).

In essence, Monty is saying that his self-concept is one of a black man, distinct and separate. Mort angrily tells Monty that nineteenty-century white domination and slavery suffuses Monty's consciousness. This frightens Monty. When Mort says that Monty loves Marx, Freud, and Einstein, all of whom are Jews, Monty replies that Mao, Fanon, and Voodoo are his new idols. With Mort's final insult, "You're freaky for JESUS" (p. 43), Monty beats him unconscious.

The other characters stir, as if from a marijuana-induced dream. Time seems to have changed once again; Monty indicates that it is now the early sixties. Everyone decides to leave the party, either to go to bed or to go home. Rick is going to the ghetto. Only Janie remains, supposedly to learn about Monty's life. Monty asks Rick to throw out Mort, which he and Flossy proceed to do. Thus ends the penultimate section.

At the beginning of *section twelve*, everyone has left the party and the scene takes on conditions reminiscent of the prologue. The only difference is that Janie's hair is combed out and she is wearing her glasses, making her all the more seductive to Monty. Contrary to what he said earlier in the play, Monty says: "I never knew it would come to this" (p. 44). Janie agrees that Monty's raping her after thirteen years of friendship is a shock. She expresses regret for the loss of friendship his behavior has brought. When she asks if he wants her to bathe, he simply begins to remove her clothes. She speaks of a friend of theirs who hanged herself, who resignedly gave in to death. Janie will not fight Monty because she knows him so well. She, like their friend, will give in to this inevitable ending, this symbolic death of their long friendship. Monty begins undressing her and declares his lust. Symbolically speaking of herself, she again mentions their friend: "She just put the noose over her head and felt her spirit dance away" (p. 45). Janie accepts the inevitable, but she is sad in her realization that this is the death of her only link with meaningful life, her platonic relationship with Monty. Monty now pushes her back and proceeds to tear off the rest of her clothes. The lights go down as the play ends.

The play's surface action defies simple analysis. A black man has raped a white woman. He has waited a long time to do so and, presumably, the intervening period in their lives and the intervening occurrences in the play help us to understand this action. However, Bullins only leads; he does not explain or define. What seems likely is that Janie wanted only a platonic friendship; however, Monty, who continuously called her "Miss Janie," an insulting name, has had a need to dominate and humilate her. Perhaps Janie represents the American ethos, to which the suppressed black has strongly ambivalent feelings. Perhaps she also represents American liberalism, with its abstract support of, yet ultimate aloofness from, the black. Since Monty, as a black American, feels that he has always been an excluded being, a second-class citizen, he has come to define his worth in terms of his ability to "make it" within, and even despite, the predominantly white cultural ethos. Although that ethos may be shallow or hollow, it must be dominated or manipulated before the black can feel triumphant.

Such attitudes, Bullins suggests, have deleterious effects on individuals and on relationships. Blacks cannot accept other blacks as desirable life partners, and true friendship between a black and a white is made difficult, if not impossible. This leads to a certain isolation for the white person who is caught in the midst of the American ethos, and a certain anger in the black who resents being riveted to the golden chains of the American dream.

It is appropriate that Bullins expresses this black/white conflict in sexual terms; miscegenation is the great fear of the racist black or white, and a false eugenics—one based on color—is the primary means by which distinction, separation, and hierarchy are maintained. Moreover, the stereotype of the vulnerable white female goddess and the supersensual black male is characteristic of American racism.

Of course, this explanation is highly speculative; the play is not a racial statement, but a vivid and truthful, if often superficially contradictory, series of impressions. Although the subject of the play is surely black/white relations in America, its intention is to present the entire racial panorama of the sixties, not to digest, differentiate, collate, or finally explain it.

At one point in the play, Rick states that this is a play about Monty's desire to rape the blonde Miss Janie. This is superficially correct; but, just as Rick's narrow racist views are based on over-simplification, so, too, is his artistic judgment inaccurate. Closer to the truth is Mort's statement:

> This is a crazy scene, ain't it? An honest-to-God creepy insane looney bin. A picture of the times, I say. And you can't forgive the creator of this mess [God? America? Bullins?] for the confusion. That's what happens when you mix things up like this. It throws everything out of kilter. Jews, niggers, politics, Germans, time, philosophy, memory, theme, sociology, past, drugs, history, sex, present, women, faggots, men, dikes, phoneys, assholes . . . everything bunched up together (p. 40).

However limited he is, and however absurd his rationalizations become, Mort is right in this monologue. Presumably, the confusion of which he speaks is the situation of America in the late sixties; and Bullins has mirrored this confusion, this craziness, in the cornucopia of this play.

Another clue to the play's aesthetic is furnished by Len in his monologue. Speaking of himself as a teacher, he praises himself for having elevated Monty's tastes, especially for stimulating his interest in drama. But this is the only time we hear mention of drama in the play. When Janie first meets Monty in creative writing class, it is his *poetry*, not his dramatic writing, that attracts her. This overlapping of the two arts is a key to Bullins' method. Poetry works largely through association, through connotation; it does not usually charge forth in clear confrontation as drama does. Similarly, the conflict of Monty and Janie is only a framework through which Bullins can express the phantasmagoria, the truly poetic complexity and subtlety of black/white relations in America. The play, then, is actually a poem in dramatic form.

In this light, the time shifts; the contradictory statements; and the intermixture of naturalism/surrealism, prose/poetry, and monologue/dialogue are assets. They enable Bullins to maintain a believable surface, to penetrate the psychology and sociology of his characters and their milieu, to leap historically as he finds it appropriate to do so, and to project the inconsistencies and confusions that exist in and around our American racial struggle.

Compounding the confusion of the play is an ambivalence in Bullins himself. Although he seems to believe in the possibility of black/white harmony (the marriage of Sharon and Len and the friendship of Monty and Janie), there is no question that strains of anti-white and anti-Jewish feeling inform the play. The anti-white feeling is clear and almost constant; the anti-Jewish orientation, more subtle, is shown in the rejection of Judaism by Sharon, Lonnie, and Mort; in the shallowness of Lonnie and Sharon; in the formulized rhetoric of pathetic Mort; and in the flippant lines concerning chicken soup and bagels and lox. Despite ambivalences, it is clearly Bullins' rage at social inequity that is the seed of his artistic vision and of his play's dynamism.

   The Taking of Miss Janie is a flawed masterpiece. Nevertheless—in its breadth; its vivid dynamic action; its structural complexity; its unique use of time; and its effective marriage of diverse styles, rhythms, and moods—it deserves respect as one of the outstanding recent contributions to the American theatre.

Entwining of the Strands

   Like *Sticks and Bones* and *The House of Blue Leaves*, *The Taking of Miss Janie* is a blend of realistic, surrealistic, and Absurdist techniques; it also contains a strong, albeit more circumscribed and less precise, social protest dimension. One of the primary differences between Bullins' play and the others is that elements of fantasy, surrealistic and symbolic, serve to enhance both realistic and Absurdist modes, i.e., to expand the play's focus from a realistic personal statement to a realistic social statement and to convey the plays existential dimension as well; in *Sticks and Bones* and *Blue Leaves*, by contrast, the surrealism functions essentially as an arm of the Absurdist orientation either divorced from or oblique to the plays' realistic properties.

   On the individual character level, the realism of *Miss Janie*, while never entirely divorced from symbolic currents, is grounded in the believability of Monty, Janie, and their circle. Monty is a black man and Janie a young white woman. She is the child of wealthy, conservative parents, and he is, at least in college, a poet. They are both college students when they meet, and we continue to glimpse the ongoing relationship and movement of their lives during a thirteen-year period. During this time, both are faithful friends. Monty's supportive role to Janie is particulary apparent; he helps her through at least one of her three abortions. Although Janie seems to want only friendship from Monty, his emotional involvement in her is not merely platonic; his sexual stalking of Janie is evident, and the play is bound by the somewhat stylized and brutally naturalistic motif of his rape of her.

The relationship of Monty and Janie, while somewhat extreme in its intensity, is realistic. This realism is reflected in their dialogue—at school, at the party (the setting of most of the play), and during the episodes of their infrequent meetings in later years. Similarly, the situation and much of the dialogue of their circle are quite realistic, even that portion, like Rick's anti-white and anti-Jewish diatribes, that is angry, sick, or prejudiced. We learn of Monty's brief marriage to Peggy, followed by her marriage to a white man and her subsequent turn to Lesbianism. We learn of Monty's sexual relationship with Flossy behind Peggy's back, even during their marriage, and of Janie's long-term relationship with Lonnie, an unsuccessful jazz musician, with whom she conceived three times, each followed by an abortion. Janie's need for independence ultimately drives Lonnie away and into the Baha'i World Faith. We learn of Rick's unceasing hatred of whites, his rise to power as a Black Nationalist, and his torturing of black women. We hear of Mort Silberstein's change from a poet and civil rights activist of the 1950s to a racist junkie living off temporary fixes, and we witness the violent last step in this metamorphosis—the breakup of the long-term friendship between Mort and Monty, begun with the shouting of political slogans and ending with Monty's beating Mort unconscious. We learn also of the interracial relationship of Sharon and Len, who weather all kinds of emotional tempests, but ultimately share a surviving marriage and have a child. As a married man, Len compromises some of his revolutionary ideals to become a businessman. Their situation is a source of anxiety to Sharon, as she tells Mort, but they may represent the one dim ray of hope, from a social vantage point, of this bleak play. And, of course, we learn finally of the rape of Janie by Monty.

While all the action is believable and each person and situation is of interest in isolation, the totality of the people and situations casts the play into a social context. The people are types (just as they are individuals when regarded in isolation), and their combined and intertwined experiences provide us with a realistic picture of the decade of the sixties, with a particularly compelling elucidation of the tension-ridden, strident, chaotic relationships of blacks and whites during that period. Unquestionably, a major effect of the play's symbolism is to support, expand, and thereby transform the play's individual realisms into a panorama of the American ethos during the transition from the sixties to the seventies.

The dialogue and interaction of the initial party scene reveal that this is not simply a story about Monty and Janie, but a rendering of the lives and viewpoints of a blend of young people of the sixties, mostly inhabitants of large cities, who in their typified rhetoric and stance tend to symbolize the era itself. The rape of white girl by black man, binding the play, conveys not only personal conflict, but a larger image of social strife. The party, symbolically the meeting place and escape hatch of the young with its wine, pot, colored lights, dancing, intense dialogue, and bad trips, conveys the broadly based social condition of a tense, troubled, confused generation with ambivalent feelings and behavior between blacks and whites. This impression of social malaise, with deleterious effects upon all (and particularly upon the blacks), is intensified by the constant discussion of race, by Rick's anti-Jewish statements, by Mort's destructive self-hatred and narrowness, by Janie's oversimplified and transparent liberal idealism, by Lonnie's shallow stab at being hip, by Rick's unending anti-white diatribe that runs through the play like a refrain.

The futuristic predictions of social chaos by Len and Peggy, the troubled monologues that suggest that even the party provides no adequate consolation, and the absolutely unfettered time movement convey an image of chaos; additionally, the ambivalence and confusion projected by the characters epitomize that of their era. The panoramic movement swings from one time frame to another, from inside to outside of individual consciousness, and from episode to episode. Despite the many shifts, all episodes and monologues are bound and presumably given significance by the rape in the prologue and epilogue. This panoramic effect surely lifts the play beyond the scope of the concerns of the individuals or group, so that it becomes a multifaceted collage that includes and yet transcends all the individuals, presenting a comprehensive, raging depiction of the erratic, chaotic era.

So powerful and multidimensional is this realistically grounded and symbolically expanded social picture of American race relations of the

1960s that the play makes an impact on this basis alone; however, its vision is broader still and more profound. The social chaos depicted by Bullins is so extreme, so totally encompassing, that it transcends the limits of social formulation. It is through this breadth, intensity, and chaos that the play's fundamental Absurdist vision presents itself.

A simple reflection upon the outcome of practically every character reveals that, as Peggy generalizes, not only are the individuals failures, but the entire generation is a failure. As for the individuals, their actions within the play or in the forecasted future show that life after life is marked by failure, degeneration, and/or perversion. These individual failures combine to form a composite picture of a deeper social failure; Monty's rape of Janie, for example, indicates the ultimate, violent breach in black/white relations. The failed lives, the constant blackouts and disjointed time elements, the failure of the party to serve as an escape valve for the anxieties of the decade, and the projection of failed dreams and compromised ideals make failure the dominant motif of the play. With this dominant motif, *Miss Janie* metaphorically conveys the notion that failure is inherent in life itself, an outlook that is often projected in Absurdist drama.

The bittersweet, tragicomic characteristics and interactions—for example, Janie's blend of innocence, awkwardness, and selfishness; her sincere but futile striving for an understanding of the black ethos; and her presumptuous, teasing, yet paradoxically poignant friendship with Monty—are also characteristic of the Absurdist theatre, as are the essential timelessness of the action, the circularlity of the plot, and the episodic structure and associative developmental pattern of the action, in which characters appear almost like ghosts out of the night to reveal the conditions of their own lives. The breaking of aesthetic distance, through juxtaposition of monologue, dialogue, direct audience address, and character commentary upon the author, produces appropriate uncertainty in the audience; we are confronted with violent ambivalence, and the theme of fragmentation is presented in episodes that are themselves fragmented. The disharmony and chaos of the social situation protrayed are emphasized by the structural disharmony and chaos of the play itself.

Audience ambivalence and confusion are further exacerbated by the violence, cruelty and/or irrationality of certain characters; moreover, the audience is denied a steadfast protagonist upon whom to focus. We are confronted with Monty's disparaging epithet "Miss Janie"; Rick's insults directed at Janie at the party; Peggy and Flossy's prejudices against whites; Mort's self-condemnation and his vilification of Sharon; and Monty's physical assault upon Mort, which ends in Mort being tossed out like garbage in almost Kafkaesque fashion. Finally, there is the brutal raping of Janie in the prologue and epilogue. Added to this verbal and physical brutality is the deeper brutality of racial hatred. This ideological brutality is simultaneously communicated by both whites and blacks, with an intensity that varies, depending upon the individual and the situation; it is conveyed with raw, terrible, and uninterrupted force by Rick, the Black Nationalist.

Given the essentially brutal structural boundaries of the play and the marijuana dream atmosphere of the party, all the negativistic elements, particularly the sad and strident monologues, combine to suggest a picture of hell. In this way, the play becomes a phantasmagoria, a nightmare vision of a tortured generation caught up in the clash of destructive energies it can neither control nor really understand. Bullins' play is so negativistic that the fragile marriage of Sharon and Len seems to be the only ray of hope, despite Bullins' obvious dissatisfaction with Len's newly acquired bourgeois lifestyle. Indeed, the play's rage at impossible social conditions seems to be almost an affirmative concern in the face of the chaotic, seemingly hopeless life that the darkly impressionistic depiction of those social conditions conveys.

Like Rabe and Guare, Bullins interweaves the strains of realism and Absurdism so thoroughly that it is difficult, if not impossible, to distinguish one orientation from the other. Like *Sticks and Bones*, which focuses upon the results of the Vietnam war for its social and existential revelations, and *The House of Blue Leaves*, which employs American religion and the movies to project its vision, Bullins uses race relations of the sixties to convey an equally powerful, broad, and negative picture of the human condition. Rabe and Guare are linguistically more compelling than Bullins, as is Albee; however, Bullins, like Robert Anderson, employs highly imaginative structural techniques to convey his vision. As with Guare and Rabe, Bullins writes with a feverish intensity. Rabe employs savage irony, poetic language, pop art caricature, and surrealistic stage happenings to convey his insights; Guare relies upon considerable onomastic play, wild farce, and a charged, spare, unembellished idiom. Bullins conveys his insights largely through direct, angry statement; incredible atmospheric intensities; and experimentation with the structure of time and action. Primarily because of the simplicity of Bullins' dialogue, occasionally flavored by purple passages, his characters, in abstraction, seem somewhat more realistic than those of either Guare or Rabe. But encased as they are in Bullins' Absurdist phantasmagoria, they strike us, as do the characters of Rabe and Guare, as thoroughly integrated parts of the new and quintessentially American realistic/Absurdist theatre.

Notes

[1]Harold Clurman, "Theatre," *The Nation*, 5 April 1975, p. 414.

[2]Mel Gussow, "Stage: Bullins' *Taking of Miss Janie*," *The New York Times*, 18 March 1975, II, p. 4.

[3]Barbara Mackay, "Studies in Black and White," *Saturday Review*, 12 July 1975, p. 52.

[4]Stanley Kauffmann, "Now and Also Then," *The New Republic*, 7 June 1975, p. 20.
[5]*Ibid.*

[6]Edith Oliver, "Fugue for Three Roommates," *The New Yorker*, 24 March 1975, p. 62.

[7]Gussow, p. 4.

[8]Clive Barnes, "Theater," *The New York Times*, 5 May 1975, p. 40.

[9]Walter Kerr, "A Blurred Picture of a Decade," *The New York Times*, 11 May 1975, II, p. 5.

[10]*Ibid.*

[11]Barnes, p. 40.

[12]*Ibid.*

[13]Catharine Hughes, "White on Black," *America*, 31 May 1975, p. 427.

[14]*Ibid.*

[15]Gussow, p. 4.

[16]Charles M. Young, "Is Rape a Symbol of Race Relations?," *The New York Times*, 18 May 1975, II, p. 5.

[17]*Ibid.*

[18]T. E. Kalem, "Requiem for the '60's," *Time*, 19 May 1975, p. 80.

[19]Kauffmann, p. 20.

[20]Mackay, p. 52.

[21]Kalem, p. 80.

[22]Barnes, p. 40.

[23]Kerr, p. 5.

[24]Young, p. 5.

[25]Barnes, p. 40.

[26]Clurman, p. 414.

[27]Ed Bullins, *The Taking of Miss Janie* (unpublished). All pages cited are from this edition, available from Samuel French Publishing Company, New York.

[28]Young, p. 5.

Double Solitaire

ROBERT ANDERSON

V

A Review of the Criticism

*R*obert Anderson's *Double Solitaire* and its science fantasy companion piece, *Solitaire*, opened at the Long Wharf Theater in New Haven, Connecticut, on February 12, 1971. In this initial production, *Double Solitaire* was performed first, followed by *Solitaire*. The two plays were then produced at the Edinburgh International Festival, and opened on Broadway on September 30, 1971; in the Broadway production, the order of presentation was reversed so that *Solitaire* was performed first. Subsequently, *Double Solitaire* appeared on public television and was produced at numerous regional theatres, including the Forum Theatre in Summit, Illinois.

Critical reaction to *Double Solitaire* has been divided; most reviewers and critics agree only that it is concerned with marital difficulty and that it is superior to *Solitaire*. Critics who reviewed *Double Solitaire* affirmatively include Brendan Gill, Henry Hewes, Thomas P. Adler, T. E. Kalem, and Clive Barnes. Negative reactions came from Vivien Leone, Harold Clurman, and Catharine Hughes. The general response to the various productions and to the areas considered relevant for critical discussion (content and theme, characterizations, structure, etc.) has remained uniform over time.

Brendan Gill, in a *New Yorker* article entitled "No Place Like Home," claims that Anderson is stressing the "consolations" and uncertainties of family life in our disjointed world. He calls the theme "bleak" and compliments Anderson for handling it in a fashion that is more "sunny" than he would have thought possible. He feels that both plays have good lines—a kind of "gallows humor"—and he is unique among critics in that he finds both works likable, making no qualitative distinction between them.[1]

Henry Hewes, by contrast, does make such a distinction, claiming that *Solitaire*, the curtain raiser, not only fails itself but interferes with audience reaction to *Double Solitaire*. Although Hewes does admit that "dangers of monotony and fuzziness . . . threaten" *Double Solitaire*, he also finds "tragic recognitions that underlie the play's rational dialogue."[2] Hewes' overall judgment is that *"Double Solitaire* contains Robert Anderson's best writing to date and is, I suspect, a better play than the Broadway version makes it seem."[3]

Thomas P. Adler, a professor at Purdue University, agrees with Hewes, suggesting that *Double Solitaire* is "probably [Anderson's] finest achievement (certainly his most original) since *Tea and Sympathy* twenty years ago," and that its principal subject is an exploration of "a marriage-on-the-rocks."[4] From Anderson's treatment of this subject, Adler extrapolates a major theatrical statement: Anderson is showing that a "man's failure to leave behind his childish romanticism will eventually destroy a marriage." Adler is here referring to Charley's desire to find again an earlier sexual union and emotional commitment in a twenty-three-year-old marriage that has lost its fire. Finding fault in Charley's romanticism, Adler asserts that Anderson's sympathy is with Barbara, Charley's wife, rather than with Charley himself. Furthermore, Adler criticizes the Forum Theatre production for distorting Anderson's vision in this regard. By finding Barbara's point of view central to Anderson's conception, Adler shares with Vivien Leone, critic for *Drama and Theatre*, a judgment that Robert Anderson is really a feminist writer, or at least somewhat sensitive to the woman's point of view. Adler puts it as follows:

> For over two decades now, from Laura in *Tea and Sympathy* to Barbara in *Double Solitaire*, Anderson has created women in the mold of Ibsen's Nora. Some slam the door on their husbands; others stay, if only temporarily. But hardly a one is a merely passive sex object when the curtain falls.[5]

Whereas Adler's ideological assessment simply reveals one of many criteria for his overall enthusiasm for the play, Leone is grateful for Anderson's "honesty," yet calls *"Solitaire . . . Double Solitaire* a pair of really quite *poor* one-act plays."[6]

T. E. Kalem's review in *Time* is more positive. In an article entitled "Who Killed the Bluebird?," Kalem compliments Anderson for his humanity, his honesty, and his gentility:

Behind the talk of loss and emptiness, there is a voice that speaks more tell-ingly than talk. It is that of Robert Anderson, best known for *Tea and Sym-pathy*. It is literate. It is—horrors!—the voice of a gentleman, someone who has been taught from childhood to uphold certain standards of decency.[7]

Clive Barnes, in reviews of both the Long Wharf and Broadway productions of the play, concurs with Kalem about its honesty. In the Long Wharf review he calls *Double Solitaire* "a naturalistic play about the erosion of marriage," and states that this work "hits harder and deeper than any play Mr. Anderson has so far written."[8] In the subse-quent Broadway review he writes:

[Anderson maintains] the warm sentiment and good-natured wit of his popular successes . . . but *Double Solitaire* takes a clearer, harsher view of humanity in its wry analysis of a marriage crumbling on the rocks.

* * *

The style is at times too glib, but the story has a tinkle of truth to it, and its ir-resolute resolution has honesty.[9]

Like Hewes and Adler, Barnes finds *Double Solitaire* to be far superior to *Solitaire* and concludes that "this simple double bill seems to me to be his finest achievement to date."[10]

As mentioned earlier, Harold Clurman does not share such ad-miration for the play. Writing in *The Nation*, Clurman concurs that:

[Anderson is] an honest man. His heart is in the right place. He is moreover a respectable craftsman, who writes effectively and unpretentiously about things that genuinely concern him.[11]

However, when comparing these plays with Anderson's earlier works, he claims that the duo is "unfortunately his weakest work." Although *Double Solitaire* comes closer than *Solitaire* to subject matter characteristic of Anderson, the play is marred, Clurman argues, by an uninteresting central chracter and the current bad habit of endless editorializing. No drama is created when characters merely analyze themselves to one another. "Doing so, they bore us and themselves to distraction."[12]

Equally ambivalent in her reaction to Anderson is Catharine Hughes, who writes in *America*:

[*Solitaire/Double Solitaire*] has its heart in the right place. . . . It is honest, occa-sionally poignant, an evening of serious purpose and fleeting humor and, in its way, uncompromising. . . . But it is also tiresome, tedious and ultimately un-successful.[13]

Although she finds Anderson's characters true and therefore touching, she finds that they lack drama, color, and vitality. In their willingness to settle for so little, they are ordinary. Like Clive Barnes, she feels the characters are not "interesting"; to Hughes, this criticism is apparently more serious. Given Anderson's alleged failures of imagination, Hughes feels that the characters and play are doomed. Although both plays are carefully written and well crafted, they are ultimately bland and unexciting.[14]

Of all the reviews of the play, Walter Kerr's is the most balanced. Although his overall judgment is negative, he clearly projects his respect for Anderson's achievement in *Double Solitaire*. His review's rhetorical title, "It's All True, But Is The Truth Enough?," foreshadows its argument. Like Clurman and Hughes, Kerr feels that the play is nondramatic; however, his reasoning is slightly different:

What is good about *Double Solitaire* is that virtually everything in it is true. What is less good about it, is that everything in it is *only* true.[15]

Calling the work "familiar beyond eavesdropping, factual short of cliché," Kerr also compliments Anderson's carefully written, open-minded, and nonsentimental treatment of the characters and their situation. He agrees in essence with Clurman that "the piece isn't meant to move. It is meant to reflect upon a movement that has ceased." But he goes on to say that "*Double Solitaire* doesn't enter its [characters'] lives." The characters "have, in a sense, been too universalized, made too perfectly typical and too statistically true, to disturb us *as persons*." Though Anderson has been "desperately honest" in *Double Solitaire*, the play does not manage to call forth our emotions; it is analytical rather than dramatic and, therefore, ultimately unsuccessful in the opinion of Kerr.[16]

While the content of Anderson's play has received most of the attention in the criticism, some important commentary has also been made on the structure of the work. Thomas Adler, for example, has alluded to the simplicity of Anderson's presentation, calling it "a return to the 'platform and a passion or two' of Elizabethan times and to the straightforward form of the Morality."[17] Henry Hewes and Walter Kerr also comment on the simple structure; Hewes notes that "all of these conversations [between Charley or Barbara and various other individuals] are preparatory to the play's ultimate dramatic confrontation [between Charley and Barbara]."[18] In his Long Wharf review, Clive Barnes also suggests that the play's structure is simple by referring to the duo as "a simple double bill" and in saying glibly that Mr. Anderson "is a fluent advocate of that maligned form, the well-made play."[19] In Barnes's Broadway review, which appeared months later, he seems more positive:

> The structure of the play is a series of sharp, short sketches, meant to display the situation and ending with a dialogue that is to resolve what two lonely people feel about their marriage. It is a *strange structure*, yet it works. At the end you know something about these unhappy refugees from the sexual revolution.[20]

In essence, disagreement over the play's structure—while it is less extensively considered than content or overall quality—mirrors the differences on the larger issue of quality. Most of the critics seem to agree that Anderson writes with honesty and a kind heart. Moreover, with the exception of Vivien Leone who pans the play, they believe that *Double Solitaire* displays Anderson's typically careful craftsmanship. The disagreements have to do with his characterization, imagination, and overall dramatic movement. Some find his characters lifeless, his situations and attitudes banal, and his drama static and analytical rather than interactive and progressive. In contrast, supporters praise him for his insight, honesty, structural complexity, humanity, and gentility. Whether the play's judgments/questions (e.g., Is marriage a bad institution?) are universal, symptomatic of our culture and our time, or particular only to these characters, is also a moot point that the critics raise but do not thoroughly answer. Finally, while Henry Hewes calls Charley the central character of the play, Thomas Adler and Vivien Leone emphasize the shift in centrality to Barbara. As Leone states, "After a whole play during which she has listened to others, it is she who does the summation."[21] Therefore, the question of who is the central character of *Double Solitaire* also remains a contested judgment by the critics and reviewers.

A Discussion

In *Double Solitaire*, a play that many critics believe to be his best, or at least his best since *Tea and Sympathy*, Robert Anderson makes his most trenchant and personal statement on marriage. The play centers on Charley and Barbara Potter, who must decide whether or not to

renew their marriage vows on their twenty-fifth anniversary, as
Charley's parents, Ernest and Elizabeth Potter, had done twenty-five
years before. The occasion for the decision is the forthcoming fiftieth
wedding anniversary of the elder Potters. The elder Potters would feel
proud, would perhaps receive a kind of *Good Housekeeping* Seal of Ap-
proval on their own marriage if their children would assert this same
gesture of faith in marriage. The request by the parents, made in-
dividually to Barbara by Mrs. Potter and to Charley by his aggressive
father, precipitates a crisis, a crisis already long in preparation in the
lives of Barbara and Charley.

The question that informs the entire play is: Will Barbara and
Charley stay together or separate? In essence, this is what their decision to renew or not renew their vows would mean. The deeper question raised is: What kind of an institution is marriage? Is it good or bad
inherently? Is it good for some but not for others, and, if it can be good,
does its goodness last?

As the curtain rises, Barbara, age forty-one, is sitting at stage left;
Charley, age forty-three, is sitting at stage right. The stage is bare with
the exception of a round table and two chairs at each side. The elder
Mrs. Potter enters, speaks with Barbara, and walks off into the
shadows. Mr. Potter then enters and speaks to Charley; within the
dialogue, the elder Mr. Potter's speeches are often long enough to be
considered monologues. In each case the elder person tells the younger
of marital incompatibility and adjustments. The elder Potters reveal
that they play double solitaire and fill their lives with a round of activities that prevent personal isolation. Mrs. Potter enjoys her poetry
readings, her garden, her sewing, and her church work. Such preoccupying activities enable her to sum up with: "We have a good life" (p.
40).[22] Mr. Potter, who seems less sanguine about life, advises "the
answer is accept the situation and find your own way to make it
work. . . . And don't ask too many questions . . . it gets worse" (p. 45).
He further advises Charley to "find some committees" (p. 47) to use up
time and energy. He himself has used clubs and committees, organiza-
tions that hold no interest for him, to "coast" along through a boring
and unfulfilling marriage.

While many facets of the elder Mr. Potter's marital life have been
unsatisfactory, his sex life has been a major source of dissatisfaction.
When she reached menopause, his wife put an end—absolute and com-

plete—to their sexual relations. Since he continued to need sexual activity, he proudly declares, this denial by his wife was extremely difficult to bear. He feels that she lacks not only sexual desires but, more importantly, a romantic spirit. For example, when he tried to take Mrs. Potter to a hotel, she thought it was silly since they had an apartment of their own.

For her part, Mrs. Potter feels that, like most men, her husband has been overly concerned with sex and romance. He has continually wanted to leave suburbia and move to a farm. She sees this idea as unrealistic escapism, saying:

> Of course he forgets the mosquitoes. Men always forget the mosquitoes . . . I do hope they've removed Thoreau from school reading lists. The image of that dreadful shack at Walden has made more men unhappy and wrecked more marriages (p. 39).

Despite their admitted incompatibilities, both Potters wish that their son and daughter-in-law would stay together. They feel that one must work to maintain a marriage, often in the face of unsatisfactory conditions. They feel that reaffirming their vows helped them twenty-five years ago and that their son and his wife could also gain comfort from such a cementing ritual.

After this parallel advice-giving process, there is another monologue, by Barbara's friend Sylvia, and then a series of dialogues (including some long, nervous speeches) until the end of the play. As the elder Mr. Potter leaves, Sylvia appears from the shadows. She is no more grounded in a particular locale than were the characters who preceded her. Moreover, she is not grounded in time. We do not know exactly when, amidst the play's imagined projection of events, her monologue is given. She may be speaking to Barbara while Charley engages in the series of dialogues that follow her appearance. Certainly, we must use the expression "cause and effect" very loosely if we are to suggest that any exclusively or even primarily logical reason accounts for Sylvia's appearing when or where she does.

Nevertheless, Sylvia's appearance is crucial and the timing of her entrance is important; the point is that nonmechanical, nonrational, very subtle, and perhaps inexpressible motivation for so including her and so timing her entrance must be sought. Since the play illustrates the ongoing conflict between Barbara and Charley, and since its action, particularly the action in the latter portion, centers upon Charley, it is important that Sylvia address Barbara first, before the whole series of scenes dominated by Charley begins. Just as Mrs. Potter's earlier remarks to Barbara served as a focus on Barbara's side of the conflict, so too does Sylvia's monologue. But whereas Mrs. Potter urged marital solidarity and the prerequisite effort, Sylvia urges an opposite alternative: divorce and freedom. Sylvia's appearance after Mrs. Potter's also parallels George's later appearance in the play, thus establishing an overall structural parallelism. Just as Mrs. Potter represents a conservative position in regard to Barbara's life orientation (i.e., coping behavior), so Sylvia represents a radical one (i.e., divorce/freedom). Mr. Potter and George, who appear in sequence, mirror that dichotomy in relation to Charley. Concomitantly, Uncle Philip, mentioned by Mr. Potter, represents freedom to Charley. Peter, who subsequently appears in a dialogue with Charley, represents true life joy. The minor characters, in this formulation, project the options open to the two leading characters and personify the evolving independent attitude fluctuations of Charley and Barbara. While this apparently neat arrangement is operative in the play and helps to explain the timing of Sylvia's entrance (i.e., as a bridge between Mr. Potter and George), it is a *complementary* structural principle, but not the *major* structural principle informing the play. While it does provide us with psychological guideposts for the play's action, the more subtle insights and overall complexity and substance of the play, including the characters' principal functions, are conveyed through a contrasting, albeit related, associative structural format. Balance, then, is one of the reasons for the appearance of Sylvia, particularly where it occurs. This is not a matter of balance in a principally mechanical sense, although there surely is a mechanical dimension to it. Rather, this balance is a mirror image of the conflict and potential dissolution of the relationship between husband and wife; this image is similar in many respects to one of an open battlefield that is perpetrated by the bare stage separating Barbara and Charley's stations of attitude.

While the play explores the conflict between Barbara and Charley, its scope is larger; it ultimately succeeds in putting all marriages on trial. In so doing, the play makes one of the most tortured, honest, and sensitive explorations of marriage in American theatre. It is in terms of this fundamental exploration, this examination of the inherent and ultimate value of marriage, that Sylvia's timeless and almost placeless appearance makes its special, and especially subtle, aesthetic contribution.

Sylvia is a woman who found that she was not well suited to marriage. While married, she was irritable, demanding, and boring, and she let herself go physically. When she broke off with her husband, she lost weight and began to feel better about herself. Since her divorce, she has seen a different man each night of the week, and not only for sex. This life has pleased her. Although friends have told her that she may be lonely when she gets older, and although she relies on a dog for companionship on Mother's Day, Christmas, and other "tribal times," she has rejected many marriage offers (all of which, she claims, were made just when the men were getting tired of making a real effort). She feels it is better to live an exciting, episodic life (despite the prospect of ultimate loneliness) than to submit to a boring exercise in mere security.

As is obvious, Sylvia, in the singularity of her monologist's role and in the content of her remarks, raises many questions that bear both on the Charley–Barbara reaffirmation decision and on the whole question of marriage itself. She intensifies the uncertainties about marriage in general and about both Potter marriages in particular. She also provides potential behavioral options for Barbara, options that remain active possibilities even after the play concludes. Sylvia's appearing from the shadows gives her an incorporeity and abstract dimension that complement the believable personal dimension of her stage appearance and her use of believable, familiar language. Sylvia's function is complex, poetic, and part of an image of overall fragmentation both in the lives of Charley and Barbara and in the institution of marriage, which George, a later character, describes as a dying institution in a period of transition.

What we have said of Anderson's portrayal of Sylvia and of his experimentation with time and setting is true of the subsequent episodes and characters as well. After Sylvia's monologue, Charley speaks in succession with his friend George, a writer whose work he edits; with his son Peter; and, finally, with his wife. While there exist many aesthetic motivations for the George conversation to precede the Peter conversation, there are no purely, or predominantly important rational ones; again, we are not absolutely certain that Charley speaks with George before he speaks with Peter or that either of these conversations occurs prior to Sylvia's monologue. So much of what occurs is part of Barbara and Charley's independent thought processes and is also part of the abstract, essentially dimensionless probing of marriage. The free, somewhat mysterious and flexible arrangement of conversational incidents mirrors the anguish of the younger Potters and permits the detailed, sinuous exploration of the larger question without creating dullness. That there is a kind of geometric balance of speeches and characters in the play provides a tension-creating superstructure that keeps us emotionally involved as we learn and assimilate details and consider theoretical questions.

Sylvia is somewhat reminiscent of Charley's Uncle Philip, to whom Mr. Potter alludes during their initial conversation. Philip has always been something of a philanderer. He has run around with many women, all beautiful, laughing women. He has no family or children, and is apparently lolling away his life on a beach in Florida. The elder Potters kept Philip away from Charley and his sister Ruth when they were children; they considered Philip a bad influence. Mr. Potter believes that Philip will suffer ultimately; actually, he hopes that Uncle Philip will suffer, because he is jealous of the free, active life Philip has led. Charley, in the conversation, declares he has always been fond of Uncle Philip. The suggestion is that he may even have had a rapport with Uncle Philip that he never had with his own father, for the next thing Mr. Potter suggests is that after the anniversary celebration is over, he and Charley should get a boat, go on a fishing trip, and get to know one another.

Sylvia and Philip have obviously led lives that seem very free and unconventional to Barbara and Charley, respectively. Charley has an additional model; his friend George has lived more freely than he. Seven years older than Charley, George declares that his "bloody footsteps" are in the sand that Charley has yet to walk. He tells Charley that he was "sick with love" for his wife when he married her; he never even considered having sex with other women. In time, however, their rapport faded and he began a series of clandestine relationships that continue in the present. Moreover, George believes that marriage will not last as an institution. He sees himself and Charley as transitional creatures in a fleeting and painful period.

It is only to his friend George that Charley is able to speak openly. He reveals that his marital relationship, and consequently his life, have lost meaning. He admits ruefully that he was nothing when Barbara met him, and that they once shared a great love and understanding; now, however, he is no longer able to communicate with Barbara. He declares he is not good as a "swinging single" and dreams of finding once more a meaningful relationship with a woman.

When George mentions Maria, a poet Charley met in California and with whom he fell in love, Charley admits his infatuation but says that the affection was essentially one-way; moreover, he never allowed the relationship to develop for fear of endangering his marriage. He could communicate with Maria, and did so in long, "adoring" letters. But he suffered tremendous guilt. Once, when he thought of sending flowers to Maria, he felt immediately guilty and bought other flowers instead, taking them home to Barbara.

Charley admits that, along with the anxiety of not knowing what to do about the wedding reaffirmation, he has also recently learned that Maria has just received a divorce and is coming East on her way to London. Charley tells George that he is not planning a rendezvous with Maria. The guilt associated with sleeping with Barbara and loving Maria had been too much for him. We never learn whether Charley does, in fact, see Maria after the play concludes.

In a "well-made play," a play of traditional structure, such strings would never remain untied. Moreover, the "well-made play" could not possibly achieve the subtle manifestation of fragmentation that so perfectly presents Charley's tortured, fragmented feelings in relation to these two women.

The fullness of the discussion, the shadowy entrance and exit of George, and the indefinite time and setting of the interaction also thrust the action well outside the rigid, rationalistic confines of a "well-made play." Of course, Charley does reveal he has proposed a trip to Barbara—and the escapade does occur in the last scene—but the uncertainty as to whether Barbara will go, the ultimate ambiguity of the final scene, and the existence of Charley's intervening scene with his son Peter, deprive even this vestigial cause and effect of its simplicity and instead make it one of the puzzle pieces of the play's grand design.

Besides balancing the Sylvia mongologue—as Sylvia and Barbara are peers, so are George and Charley—the George conversation projects the intensity of Charley's struggle, clarifies Charley's character by contrast to the less sober and less conventional George, concretizes the past and present state of Charley and Barbara's marriage, and broadens the discussion of marriage by contrasting Charley's view with that of a man who engages somewhat casually but also somewhat desperately in a series of affairs. The discussion seems to reveal marriage as a dying institution to which these unhappy characters cling; we wonder whether they will continue on or abandon it.

As the more sober Charley and the more easy-going George discuss marriage, Charley finds that in times of difficulty they have followed similar courses of behavior. He has tried some of George's gestures—expensive flowers, expensive presents, attempts to recapture the past through dancing or nightclubbing, a variety of innovative sexual exploits, and sudden trips alone to faraway places. George tells Charley that these attempts never work. The golden past cannot be re-evoked or relived.

Charley reveals two things about himself that differentiate him from George: he still finds that sex works as a means of communication when all else has failed; and also he feels, as he did even in college, that he needs to adore someone with whom he has a sexual relationship. Charley says that his family motto is *Dum spiro, spero* ("while I breathe, I hope"); as a gesture of hope, he has asked Barbara to go off to a secluded beach with him to try to recapture the ecstasy of their first sexual encounter. She has put him off because of her preoccupation with the many preparations for the anniversary celebration, but Charley declares that he believes she would go if he insisted. The prospect is there, therefore, of a desperate and perhaps fruitful attempt at their emotional reunion. However, as he parts from George, it is clear that his father's request has brought a serious problem to the surface and upset him considerably.

Following the conversation between editor Charley and writer George—Charley himself had once tried to be a writer, but without sufficient and sustained commitment because he also tried to be a family man—the play continues its experimentation with time and setting by presenting a conversation between Charley and his twenty-one-year-old son, Peter. That Peter, as a film-maker, is artistically inclined emphasizes, as did George's writing talent, the contrast between Charley, as editor, and these minor characters. Charley has relinquished the more passionate, creative life of artist in favor of a more secure role as editor. Peter shows Charley a three-minute film he has recently made about his joyful return home from work to his beloved Melinda, who is shown taking a bath. The film shows him fondling Melinda and leaves them in joyful physical play. Anderson's use of film continues a photography motif that runs through the entire play. For example, after going with Peter and Melinda to The Electric Circus, the older Mr. Potter has decided to have wedding films of his friends projected on the walls during his fiftieth anniversary celebration. There is also the reference to Charley's having sold his stories to the movies, to Mr. Potter's interest in cameras, to Mrs. Potter's not being photogenic, and to children who see former pictures of their parents when they were young and in love. The emphasis on photography symbolizes the desperate attempt of people to preserve what is beautiful and meaningful in life. Life is short and pleasures are few and fleeting, but the camera, through its illusion, can seem to make time stand still and to offer the assurance that pleasure has never left us or will never fade.

Essentially, the interchange between Peter and his father centers on Peter's criticism that his father's generation is artificial. More precisely, Peter feels that married people of his father's generation do not love each other. They are unfaithful and do such awkward, crazy things as drinking wildly, switching wives, or pushing each other into swimming pools to feel alive. Peter wants none of this artificiality in his life; he wants to freeze time with Melinda—to remain passionate, unmarried, and childless. He will never, like his father, drink martinis in order to have sex; he will never submit to a dull routine. He feels that his parents should have gotten a divorce long ago instead of staying together for the children. To Peter, the real element in his father's stories has been the "ache and longing and pain" (p. 65), not the false justifications for marriage.

In answer, Charley tells his son not to judge his generation too harshly for trying to sustain themselves. He also says that children have traditionally disparaged the relationships of their parents and asserts that he, too, as a young college student believed in and wrote of passionate love and protested against the establishment.

Charley finds Peter's attitudes toward passion vs. marriage naive and overly simplistic. He resents Peter's criticism, saying:

> . . . I hope to Christ you do [end up differently]. But you do not have a patent on the search for meaningfulness in life or love. . . . The middle-aged man is much more fed up with things than you are. And he's in a much worse spot, because he can't feed himself simple solutions, because he knows they won't work. He's got the same anguish, but no clear answers, and time is running the hell out on him. And while he's desperately trying to salvage something before it's too late, the kids sneer at him and say, "You sold out. You blew it." And then he says to them, because he's hurt, "Wait till it's your turn!" (pp. 66–67)

He hopes that Peter and Melinda *will* find a lasting relationship and swears that he will do whatever he can to help them, but he remains skeptical that such naive, pure joy can survive. The dialogue ends with the showing of Peter's film. It affects Charley by its beauty and its unaffected sensual joy and youth; however, it also makes him sad, for he senses how much joy has been lost in his own life.

Critical in our involvement in the Peter–Charley interaction is the sense that Peter and Melinda are people with a distinct lifestyle and specific new problems. They are not simply appendages of the Potters or elementary illustrations of the premarital situation and ideals of the Potters. Peter, as Charlie indicated, is vulnerable to potential problems. As such, he is similar to George, battered in marriage, but unfulfilled in extramarital affairs; Sylvia, free but lonely; and the elder Potters, together but preoccupied with their individual interests and their "double solitaire" adjustment. Once again, in the fullness of its characterization and the variety, richness, and depth of its human concerns, Anderson's play runs directly counter to the practice of the "well-made play."

Whether or not Peter's film has perpetrated Charley's encouraging Barbara to an attempted renewal of their love, in the next and final sequence Barbara and Charley are at a secluded beach, the hideaway spot he mentioned to George. In essence, Charley makes every effort to arouse Barbara sexually, and she just as strongly tries to dampen his enthusiasm. We wonder what the sexual result will be and how it will affect their marriage.

Following an interminable sexual banter—Charley trying to advance and Barbara parrying—Charley gets serious, reminding Barbara that they have had no sex in a long time; she blames her lack of interest on the exhaustive preparations for the anniversary party. She then opens the large question of their relationship; in a long speech, she claims that, except for physical contact for which he has to take martinis, they have entirely lost touch with each other. Barbara declares she hates marriage, for it has made her less "loving, warm, generous, and understanding" (p. 80). She says that while Charley likes marriage as an institution, he cannot accept its placidities, and she cannot satisfy or respond to his need for intensity. In fact, his demands for passion have frightened her and made her withdraw. Moreover, she thinks they have nothing in common and that twenty-three years together is a ridiculously long time; she has been considering a divorce. After telling him how lonely she has been and how she hates his desperate love behavior, she repels his advance. However, Charley persists, and, although she at first discourages him ("You won't find anything there you haven't found a thousand times before"—p. 83), she finally smiles sadly and touches his head. Structurally, this onslaught by Barbara constitutes a startling change. Until this scene, the play concentrated on Charley; matters had been seen from his perspective, and we empathized with him. Through this radical shift in the concluding scene, Anderson has endowed his play with an admirable balance and made his exploration of marital dynamics considerably more profound. This is a muticlimax drama of a troubled male, Charley, seeking female solace. But it is also a dual-focus play, with a hidden dramatic gem, Barbara's perspective, saved for and revealed at the conclusion.

Just before she submits, Barbara expresses uncertainty as to whether they will be together two years hence. Therefore, the play leaves many questions unresolved; most importantly, we are left to ponder its central dramatic question: will or should Barbara and Charley stay together? In a "well-made play," we would be directed toward an answer. However, Anderson elects not to wrap things up so tidily. Instead, he provides us with a thorough exploration of "a marriage on the rocks" and some very trenchant criticism of the marriage institution itself. Rarely has any writer written so sincerely, so personally, and yet so dispassionately of portions of human experience that are usually hidden away and left unexplored. By doing this, he confronts pain.

Unlike the "well-made play," in which great care is expended on preparation for or foreshadowing of all future developments, *Double Solitaire* presents a series of random core incidents. Its development is not based on a "logic of events." Although it is somewhat foreshadowed, even the final scene occurs without any clear sense of inevitability; yet, it is fully within the realm of verisimilitude. No twisted incidents, no secret letters or delayed messengers mar the play; the final scene occurs gracefully, growing out of the play's total aesthetic, not out of any logical or mechanistic formula.

Whether the term "well-made play" is a useful critical conception or merely a misleading and exclusivist tag is a moot point. If we do assume that it is a formal and precise critical category, as we have hypothesized in this examination, we must surely exclude Robert Anderson's *Double Solitaire* from this category. Anderson's play is not mechanical; rationalistic; grounded simply in logic; bound by cause and effect; unidimensional; or beset by the sometimes tortured, artificial devices of playwrights intent on "well-made" works with clear, simple conclusions. Rather, it is a sensitive, multidimensional, episodic, detailed exploration of marriage as a highly troubled institution clung to by very vulnerable individuals. It is honest and direct, and it uses many experimental devices to move itself along. As Anderson himself has said:

> This is not a "well-made play." The structure is far more complex than that term would suggest. Into the play *Double Solitaire*, I put everything I knew about playwriting.[23]

Besides being a playwright of renown, a teacher of playwriting, and a script writer for radio and films, Anderson is a student of English letters who is certainly aware of traditions. These facts alone ought to discourage an application of the "well-made play" rubric; *Double Solitaire* is an experiment in dramaturgy, drawing upon and blending many of the techniques of the past and adding some truly novel touches as well. More experimental than the actual structure is the the subject itself; Anderson's exploration of love and marriage is unique in its depth and honesty. The playwright who first treated homosexuality on the American stage, who preceded and foreshadowed the existence and comicality of the Theater of Nudity, who showed that polite conversation can still form the heart of dramatic experience in *Silent Night, Lonely Night*, and who demonstrated that a keen comic skill also lay within his ken in *You Know I Can't Hear You When the Water's Running*, has made an important and truly innovative contribution to dramaturgy in *Double Solitaire*.

Entwining of the Strands

Double Solitaire is the most directly and consistently realistic of the five plays treated in this study. The appearance, behavior, and dialogue of the characters are entirely realistic, as are the matter, if not the manner, of the monologues by Mrs. Potter and Sylvia. Furthermore, the play's content, the general situations and conditions of the characters, is also entirely familiar and believable, although it is a reality that is subtly intensified.

The focus in this one-act play is on a middle-aged couple at a time of crisis. They are trying to save their marriage, or at least to combat the sense that their relationship (and consequently, their lives) has lost its meaningfulness.

In realistic fashion, Anderson's play focuses on a particular event, the forthcoming fiftieth wedding anniversary celebration of Charley's parents. The elder Potters are planning a gala affair, highlighted by a four-screen projection of home movies and slides, of their own marriage, their son's marriage, and the marriages of some of their friends. The elder Potters also want the celebration to include a re-enactment of wedding vows by Charley and Barbara, who are celebrating their twenty-fifth anniversary. The elder Potters had themselves re-enacted their own vows twenty-five years before. The pivotal question of whether Charley and Barbara will choose to reaffirm their vows constitutes the primary dramatic question of the play; the question is discussed by Charley with his father and with George, by Barbara with Mrs. Potter, and by the couple themselves. This question (and the deeper question of whether the couple will remain together) gives a plot-like frame to the play, endows it with subterranean energy, and engenders the discussion of marriage and the broader discussion and concern over the meaning and value of life itself.

Both questions are realistic, as are the characters who are involved in the related conflicts. Like many old people, the elder Potters wish their children to follow traditional life patterns, similar to those they themselves followed. They urge such established patterns because they are anxious for their children's welfare, but an even stronger motivation is their need to reaffirm the patterns. Friend George (whose marriage has lost its vitality) and Sylvia (now divorced and living a somewhat escapist existence, seeing a different man each night) are thoroughly believable individuals and types. Peter, believing feverishly in love, rejecting marriage, and feeling that his parents' generation has failed, is also realistic. Charley, who is married but infatuated with another woman, and Barbara, who has seriously considered divorce, are similarly real; so is the totality of their environments, past and present. Even the decision as to whether to remain together—raised directly in the play's final scene—is both a recognizable symptom of our age and a realistic outgrowth of the specific Charley–Barbara situation.

As well as being realistic, the presentation of the characters' lives is decidedly negativistic. The old people rely on double solitaire to pass the time together; George cheats on his wife; Sylvia is involved in several concurrent affairs; and Peter, who is not formally married but very much in love, seems to be living an illusion. The cyclical pattern portrayed and discussed suggests that young love cannot survive marriage; married life often brings disaffection, disappointment, or divorce. Couples who do remain together do so with sad resignation and preoccupying diversions (e.g., double solitaire, which the elder Potters suggest to Charley and Barbara). The cyclical pattern suggests inevitability—the death of young love, happiness, closeness, and creative and meaningful life.

Related to this negativistic life pattern are the play's concerns with aging and escapism. The play suggests that we pursue activities not because of their intrinsic value, but because such activities can divert our attention, pass time, and thereby obscure grim reality. If we do not dwell on misery, we might not feel miserable; like the elder Potters, we might not perceive our routine as a death-in-life state.

Were the considerations of this world of unhappy marriages and frustrated lives insufficient to categorize the play as partially Ab-

surdist, the presentational mode of the play assures such categoriza-
tion. Its theatrical manner, if not its matter, is certainly an offshoot of
European Absurdism. First, the bare stage with few properties serves
to isolate the characters, to set them beyond the boundaries of individual personality and outside the protective confines of home and
hearth. In this bare setting, the various characters drift in and out;
their interactions are episodic and often, as in the case of Mrs. Potter
and Sylvia, involve long monologues that emphasize isolation. In
dialogues, many of the speeches are also quite lengthy, serving to
isolate the characters even further.

This isolation is made particularly dark and terrible—almost
nightmarish—by the manner in which the characters appear. At the
play's outset we have two round tables, each with two chairs; Charley
sits at one table, stage right, and Barbara sits at the other, stage left.
The physical separation of the two characters is striking and dramatic,
for it emphasizes the separation of their attitudes. Further, the absolute balance of the set, dark and bare, suggests that they are locked
into the isolated condition in which we encounter them. With this initial isolation established, the elder Mrs. Potter appears from the
shadows to address Barbara. Mrs. Potter's long initial monologue
seems as much an isolated self-address as it does an interchange with
Barbara. After Mrs. Potter speaks to Barbara, she moves back into the
shadows, followed in a similar pattern by Mr. Potter (to Charley),
Sylvia (to Barbara), George (to Charley), and Peter (to Charley). The
last scene, after the showing of Peter's joyful film, begins with Charley
and Barbara intently gazing at each other from their separate tables.
Charley then moves his chair to the center of the stage and Barbara
slowly follows suit, after which the final scene, the only scene in which
the major characters really communicate, unfolds. Because the
characters appear in no precise time sequence, but rather in the
associative pattern characteristic of Absurdist drama, and because of
the darkness and shadows that confine, obscure, accompany, and in-
fuse their appearances and actions, they take on a certain ghostlike
quality; as suggested earlier, this abstract time scheme and continual
darkness and isolation consequently endow the play with the atmosphere of a disturbing dream.

The flat screen, which sits on the stage from the outset; the showing of slides and films; and the overall emphasis on photography (i.e., living life through pictures and viewing pictures shown in darkness) convey even further the notion that the lives of the characters are un-fulfilled and enveloped by darkness. Peter and Melinda are, of course, the superficial exception, but they are caught, willy-nilly, in the elementary stage of the negative cyclical pattern of their parents and grandparents.

Double Solitaire never answers its primary dramatic question; we do not know if Charley and Barbara will renew their vows at the an-niversary celebration. Whether or not they do, we know that the celebration is itself a coverup for an unpleasant set of conditions; with or without the superficial ritual, their marriage is terribly fragile. Since that marriage gives meaning and order to their lives, it mirrors the con-tingent condition of their lives, and perhaps of everyone's life.

Double Solitaire depicts a marriage on the rocks. With absorbing sensitivity, it realistically projects the outward lives, the inner psychology, and the unspoken attitudes of its characters. Because the characters are so troubled and because their plight seems so in-escapable and typical, we feel that the play is no mere human interest story; rather, in typical Absurdist fashion, it evolves as a negative com-ment on the human condition—a condition that tends to be both fragile and meaningless. The play's nontraditional structure, its sparse set-ting, its associative developmental pattern, its dark and shadowy at-mosphere, its isolating monologues and picture sequences, and its sad comedy are similarly and concomitantly negativistic. The dark em-phasis with which Anderson endows his realistic revelation of the marital embroilment of Charley and Barbara transforms this work from a compelling psychological and social document into a philosophically absorbing life canvas. In other words, the Ibsenite strand of realism has been gracefully entwined with the technical elements, dramatic strategy, and dark philosophy derived from the European Absurdists.

[1]Brendon Gill, "No Place Like Home," *The New Yorker*, 9 October 1971, p. 95.

[2]Henry Hewes, "A Husband's Undoing," *Saturday Review*, 16 October 1971, p. 35.

[3]*Ibid.*

[4]Thomas P. Adler, "Theatre in Review," *Educational Theatre Journal* (December 1974), pp. 529-530.

[5]*Ibid.*

[6]Vivien Leone, "Notes From an Accidentally Passionate Playgoer," *Drama and Theatre*, 10 (1971-1972), p. 134.

[7]T. E. Kalem, "Who Killed the Bluebird?," *Time*, 11 October 1971, p. 74.

[8]Clive Barnes, "Stage: Long Wharf Takes Wry Looks at Marriage," *The New York Times*, 2 March 1971, p. 29.

[9]Barnes, "Theater: Anderson's *Solitaire, Double Solitaire*," *The New York Times*, 1 October 1971, p. 33.

[10]Barnes, "Long Wharf," p. 29.

[11]Harold Clurman, "Theatre," *The Nation*, 18 October 1971, p. 380.

[12]*Ibid.*

[13]Catharine Hughes, "*Solitaire/Double Solitaire*," *America*, 23 October 1971, p. 322.

[14]*Ibid.*

[15]Walter Kerr, "It's All True, But Is The Truth Enough?," *The New York Times*, 10 October 1971, II, pp. 1, 3.

[16]*Ibid.*

[17]Adler, p. 529.

[18]Hewes, p. 35.

[19]Barnes, "Long Wharf," p. 29.

[20]Barnes, "Theater," p. 18 (emphasis added).

[21]Leone, p. 136.

[22]Robert Anderson, *Solitaire/Double Solitaire* (New York: Random House, 1971). All pages cited are from this edition.

[23]Telephone conversation with Anderson in early 1976.

Seascape

EDWARD ALBEE

VI

A Review of the Criticism

*M*ixed critical reaction has greeted Edward Albee's *Seascape*. Such critics as Clive Barnes, George Oppenheimer, Richard Watts, and Brendan Gill have written of their admiration for the work; others, including Walter Kerr, T. E. Kalem, Stanley Kauffmann, Jack Kroll, and Catharine Hughes, have been equally emphatic in deriding it. Harold Clurman, who scorns the hysteria of the love or hate reaction of his colleagues, has a generally favorable reaction to the play. Although he calls it a "little" play, his tone indicates that he is surely among that group of critics who might "find [the work] delightful."[1]

Mel Gussow, in a *New York Times* interview with Albee, reports that Albee began to think about *Seascape* in 1967, seven years before it was produced. It grew out of one of two companion pieces, at that time called *Life* and *Death*. *Death* ultimately became *All Over*, produced in 1971, and *Life* became *Seascape*, to which Albee gave special attention for three years prior to its writing.

Gussow finds in *Seascape*, as in most of Albee's works, elements of both tragedy and comedy. During the interview, Albee credits Samuel Beckett with traits that may be credited to himself as well:

> Our best serious playwright, Samuel Beckett, is extremely funny. You've got to have a tragic sense of life to see the humor of the absurd.[2]

As the Gussow interview indicates, Albee was indeed quite serious in this dramatic effort. He allegedly has always been fascinated by the sea; in addition, he read extensively in anthropology and animal behavior in preparation for the writing. However, Albee does not see simple scientific knowledge as his substructure. Gussow calls it "still very much a play of the imagination." Albee states that it was the most difficult play he has ever written because he had no guidelines and because language and diction were particularly acute problems. He had to make the lizards seem believable and yet decidedly different from humans. As Albee states:

> They should be so real that in a sense we can smell them. They should be quite frightening. Seeing them for the first time, the audience should have that shock of recognition. After all, it's what we all were.[3]

However charming or witty the play might be, the Gussow interview indicates that Albee was attempting to confront weighty scientific and philosophical matters and to treat them in a fundamentally serious, though overtly whimsical, fashion.

It is precisely because of the seriousness of Albee's aim and posture that most of the criticism of the play has been leveled. In essence, a number of critics feel that *Seascape* is pretentious, dull, and pseudophilosophic; talky when it ought to have provided action; and abstract and distant when it ought to have conveyed intense feeling. Quite pointedly, T. E. Kalem of *Time* states that since *Who's Afraid of Virginia Woolf*, Albee's plays (including *Seascape*) have been "flaccidly somnolent affairs." Claiming that Albee has "a very weak gift for plot construction," he scores the characterization and language, refers to the play's "thudding banalities," and calls the work "bland and innocuous, a two-hour sleeping pill of aimless chatter."[4] Similarly, Jack Kroll of *Newsweek* writes that Albee "seems drained of almost all vitality—theatrical, intellectual, artistic." Moreover, Kroll thinks that Albee has "committed the grisly error of becoming a 'sage.' "[5]

Catharine Hughes, who agrees with Kalem and Kroll that the play lacks "life," states:

> As a course in elementary Darwinism, *Seascape* just might have some value. As a play, it is pretentious, simplistic, verbose and banal.[6]

Essentially in agreement, Stanley Kauffmann calls it hollow, banal, and unrealized. He goes on to suggest that Albee give up playwriting, since he has allegedly produced nothing of worth since *Virginia Woolf*.[7] In a more moderate but equally firm critique, Walter Kerr argues that the play fails principally because it is not dramatic. The play begins with a long conversational debate between the middle-aged couple, Charlie and Nancy. In retirement, Charlie wants only to rest, while Nancy wants wonder and excitement. The couple is joined by two sea creatures, with whom they compare notes on many facets of their lives. When the sea creatures decide—inevitably, Kerr contends—to return to the sea, we have a crisis, but Kerr believes that Albee fails to present this crisis effectively. Since Charlie had formerly wished to surrender to old age and death, Kerr asks, "Why does he not engage himself, as devil's advocate, as newly enlightened human being, as something?"[8]

While the questions of dramatic effectiveness, philosophical richness, construction, and vitality are surely points of disagreement among critics, nowhere is the debate so pointed and acrid as it is on the subject of Albee's language. For example, T. E. Kalem writes:

> Finally, he largely abandoned his strong suit, which was a flair for vituperatively explosive dialogue and bitchy humor. Instead, his characters have spoken for years now with intolerably stilted pomposity, as if they had wandered out of an unpublished work by some minor Victorian novelist.[9]

Similarly, Kroll censures Albee's "constipated language that moves in colonic spasms."[10] Catharine Hughes, another detractor, states that Albee's writing "is presumed (by the author) to be poetic and profound, resonant, when in reality it is devoid of life and artificial, the producer of inertia."[11]

Although such judgments on Albee's language are powerful, they are not universally held. For example, Walter Kerr comments:

> The writing is blessedly spare, free of the convoluted locutions that have sometimes grown like coral over [Albee's] meanings.[12]

Similarly, Brendan Gill writes in *The New Yorker*:

> Of all Mr. Albee's plays, *Seascape* is the most exquisitely written. He has calculated not only every immaculate line of dialogue but every word, every caesura; when the actors fall silent, we hold our breath and wait, as we wait at the reading of some superb long poem.[13]

Clive Barnes and Henry Hewes are affirmative in their overall assessment of the play. Because of its warmth and human compassion, Barnes calls *Seascape* a true comedy, "a major dramatic event," and further states: "What Mr. Albee has given us here is a play of great density, with many interesting emotional and intellectual reverberations."[14] Henry Hewes, agreeing that it is a comedy, praises Albee for his "wit," "insight," and "careful use of language." Although he believes that the first act lacks "dramatic urgency," Hewes concludes his critique by referring to *Seascape* as "a unique comedy—one that gives us more to think about than any other of this season's new plays."[15]

Harold Clurman seems to explain the differences in critical response to *Seascape*. He writes:

> It is his most relaxed play, a "philosophical" whimsy. You may find it
> delightful, or, if the nice notion on which it is based does not suit your tempera-
> ment, you will consider it a drag.[16]

The term *philosophical whimsy* suggests the light tone, the wit, and the playful creativity of language, idea, and theatrical image that Albee attempted to employ. If one disregards this graceful blending of light manner and serious matter, the work surely seems pretentious, the metaphor insoluble, and the language heavy. Seen, however, from the vantage point that Clurman suggests, we are compelled to open our minds regarding *Seascape,* as Albee suggested in an interview with the editors of *The New York Times*: "The most important thing you can ask from an audience is that it approach a new play with an open mind—without having predetermined the nature of the theatrical experience it will accept."[17]

While the detractors say little more of the play than that it is concerned with a troubled middle-aged couple and that it is concerned scientifically (or pseudoscientifically) with evolution, the play's supporters have attempted various interpretations, each more or less related to Albee's contention that the play is "a true-to-life story."[18] For example, Clive Barnes claims that the play confronts life itself—its history, processes, and current expression in the human condition—and optimistically reminds us about "the primeval ooze from which we all came, and the blind, inarticulative courage that keeps us all going."[19] Oblique but related is the interpretation of Henry Hewes:

> Albee seems to be suggesting that the real solution is for our civilization to
> recognize its failures and somehow to feed our experience into the evolution of
> a new and better species.[20]

Brendan Gill concludes:

> Boldly and simply, it asserts that, at no matter what age and in no matter what
> time and place, acts of discovery remain to be undertaken. With luck, such
> acts will be found to have meaning; better still, there is the possibility that they
> will bear fruit.[21]

Regardless of which critical opinion we adhere to, we would do well to ponder Clurman's judgment that *Seascape* "is a step in Albee's still green career, a step which, seen in a certain light, augurs well for the future."[22]

In addition to receiving the Pulitzer Prize for *Seascape*, Albee won the Elizabeth Hull–Kate Warriner Award, given by the Dramatists Guild Council, for the 1974–1975 season. This award "is given to a playwright whose work deals with a controversial subject involving political, religious or social mores."[23]

A Discussion

Edward Albee's *Seascape*, produced in 1975, won the Pulitzer Prize for that year. The tenth Albee play to be produced (the thirteenth if we include his adaptations), the work reassures us that Albee is still a powerful force in American theatre. Many critics have felt, throughout the course of Albee's career, that his most recent play would be his last. The notion that Albee had played himself out arose shortly after the production of *Who's Afraid of Virginia Woolf?*; it was repeated for the next ten years and received new support in 1971 when *All Over*, which was concerned with death, seemed to state explicitly (in its title and symbolically throughout) that this would be the last Albee play. But Albee stunned critics and audiences again in 1975 with the production of *Seascape*. Hailed by Clive Barnes as "a major dramatic event," *Seascape* is of double significance. First, it reminds us that Albee is alive and well and writing superbly. More importantly, his winning a second Pulitzer Prize (he had won it in 1966 for *A Delicate Balance*) affirmed his right to claim such a well-deserved honor, denied him for *Virginia Woolf* in 1962. (Because of the 1962 denial, John Mason Brown and John Gassner withdrew from the Pulitzer Prize Committee.)

Seascape is a two-act play concerned with a middle-aged couple, Nancy and Charlie. The setting is an isolated beach to which the couple has come for a vacation. The first act is largely a dialogue concerned with the couple's finding ways both to fill the emptiness and to combat the loneliness that have entered their lives. Basically, Nancy wants a life of excitement and new adventures, wandering from one secluded beach to another; Charlie wants simply to rest, to do absolutely nothing.

The first act begins with the deafening roar of a jet airplane passing overhead. This sound, which annoys and interrupts the couple's dialogue, is heard three times during the first act. It serves as a contrast to the quiet calm and pristine beauty of the sand dunes, and serves to remind us of the world outside the isolated beach. After the plane's initial roar passes, Nancy and Charlie debate whether to spend the remainder of their lives beachcombing and seeking adventure or to rest and let the years pass by uneventfully. Although the dialogue continues for a long time with no action, Albee keeps us absorbed in the conversation through his customary control of language. Although Nancy and Charlie speak of emptiness and inactivity, Albee's sense of verbal nuance, his ear for actual speech patterns, and his ability to heighten and intensify naturalistic speech endow the conversation with a wonderful energy. Moreover, we are drawn by the characters' situation (perhaps plight), the basic seriousness of their concerns, and the charming mixture of lightness and wit as a leaven to the sober communication.

The direct consideration of Nancy's beachcombing suggestion leads the couple to consider the meaning of life and the imminence of death. Nancy responds to Charlie's desire to rest by asking:

> But is this what we've . . . come all this way for? (*Some wonder and chiding*)
> Had the children? Spent all this time together? All the sharing? For nothing? To
> lie back down in the crib again? The same at the end as at the beginning?
> Sleep? Pacifier? Milk? Incomprehensible once more? (p. 9)[24]

This statement, coupled with Nancy's fervor in considering old age, retirement farms, and whether they will die together or alone, causes Charlie to agree smilingly to Nancy's proposition of a life of endless beachcombing; he does so principally in an effort to pacify Nancy and to rest. Just as they reach a state of relaxation, the jet plane again roars overhead. Almost ritually, Nancy repeats her initial line, which came after the plane first disturbed them: "Such noise they make!" (pp. 3, 13). The repetition is deceptive; the plane's droning actually serves as a kind of coda, leading the couple to a new area of discussion. Such a change might in fact happen quite naturally in any conversation after such a disturbance, and the purity and cleanness of the transition maintains the ritualistic quality that lies just beneath the naturalistic surface of Albee's play.

Although this new period of discussion concerns numerous subtopics, it focuses primarily upon Charlie's boyhood practice of diving underwater and staying submerged for long periods of time. Ever since

Charlie was a little child, he wished to live under the sea, and so he often would let out all the air from his lungs, sink as far down as he could, and remain there as long as possible. He loved to watch the fish and see the variegated colors of the underwater world, and presumably he felt a sense of oneness with the sea, the place from which all living creatures originally came.

In contrast to Charlie's impulse toward sea life, Nancy reveals that she wanted to be only two things when she was young: a pony and a woman. As they banter about her having achieved her second aim, they move associatively—the play's method—to the marvel of having built a family ("a reversed *pyramid*, always in danger of toppling over when people don't behave themselves"—p. 15). The challenge, excitement, and wonder of having built a family and the continuity of life are matters to which the couple thrill in discussion. Albee indicates a true reverence for the beauty of togetherness and closeness, which the word *family* implies. There is truth and tenderness between this couple; there is also love. Albee reveals himself in this discussion and throughout the play as a man of much wisdom, warmth, and insight into life.

Again, Charlie returns to a description of his submergence—this time at a protected cove at a summer place when he was a teenager. He tells how he would enter naked and remain under for a very long time, becoming "part of the undulation and the silence" (p. 17). He remembers that it "was very good" (p. 17). Appreciating the richness of Charlie's experience, with its associations of youth, courage, sensuality, and deep communion with nature, Nancy, who from the play's start has been trying to reactivate Charlie's life impulses, encourages him to strip and submerge himself once more. When he hesitates, she encourages him by countering all of his objections, including the possibility that some other beachcombers would observe him. Nancy wants him to relive the experience both for himself and for her own vicarious excitement. Since this experience has many sexual associations and ramifications, her encouragement leads them to a discussion of sex and the loss of potency. Associatively again, they go on to discuss marital fidelity and sexual fantasy.

Nancy tells of how, during a period when Charlie was melancholic, she had thought of divorcing him. She had been a modest girl before her marriage, but by marrying and staying with only one man, she feels that she deprived herself of much sexual experience. She reveals that she has dreamed of former boyfriends with whom she missed her chance for sexual involvement. She has thought of liberation and of regaining her youth by starting again. Such thinking, she contends (presumably, Albee agrees), is the cause of many divorces. Nancy's own wavering came when she was thirty; she recalls an instance when she was quite pretty, pink, and literate; propped up beside Charlie in bed, she stared at the moles on his back while he, in a state of melancholia, lay there unresponsive and uninterested in her.

At that time, Nancy had wondered if Charlie had found another woman; knowing how various are the springs of attachment, she would not have really blamed him if he had had such a relationship. Her mother, she reveals, had said that if Charlie did leave and had then returned to her, he would have done so at a price, the price being some loss of spiritual fidelity. Her mother suggested that that would bring Nancy "halfway to compassion" (p. 24). When Charlie asks what would then establish *full* compassion, Nancy answers that the other half of the journey to compassion would have had to do with sensing his loneliness and male need for liberation. In any case, she divested herself of the divorce notion within a week.

While Charlie agrees with her that fantasy can play a significant part in sexual relations, he contends that he has been faithful to Nancy, both in mind and in spirit. They now feel quite close, and Nancy again encourages him to find his cove, to submerge, even to take her along if he wishes. She looks about and says that the other sunbathers have gone; he would not be observed. This renewed exhortation by Nancy is motivated by her sense that so much in life is fleeting, "so much goes" (p. 25). She mentions her eyesight specifically, and yet implies the more intangible commodities of youth and opportunity.

Then Nancy thinks she sees people farther up on the dunes. Since she cannot see them clearly, Charlie jests that she would be of little use if they went underwater together. She comments that she would depend on Charlie's protection; this notion causes them to compliment each other on the sharing they have enjoyed as lovers and as married people. Charlie, for example, had courted her as she wished, been a good husband, and provided a "sturdy shoulder and a comfortable life" (p. 30). This sense of having wrapped life up neatly makes Nancy bridle, and she petulantly insults Charlie, saying: "We'll wrap you in the flag when you're gone, and do taps" (p. 30). This remark hurts Charlie, and he says that he wants to go home.

A recollection of a past incident, however, diverts them. Nancy recalls the time that Charlie was stung by a bee and ordered her to make mud. She recalls how, after years of working from recipes, she could not figure out the recipe for mud. She explains that her petulance comes upon her like a bee sting, calling it involuntary behavior that momentarily closes off her impulse to kindness. Charlie accepts this explanation, and she goes on to state that what most often causes her petulance is his speaking as if their lives were over.

Charlie agrees with Nancy that all they really have is "ourselves and some time" (p. 37), and once more they express their opposed attitudes: Charlie wants to rest and Nancy wants to find excitement. Charlie contends that one must face reality, the reality of death. Nancy opts for not giving up, for seeking and scaling the "glaciers and the crags" (p. 38). Slowly the debate plays itself out and they speak of returning to the business of the day—writing postcards and gathering seashells.

At this moment the act (and the play) makes its most dramatic and sensational shift. As Charlie and Nancy speak, two huge sea lizards, Leslie and Sarah, come up on the dune and squat down on their tails. Rarely in any dramatic experience, American or foreign, has fantasy been so strikingly imposed on a naturalistic environment. Actually, the imposition is merited; the couple has just been speaking of reality and illusion, and the notion that life is dull and unexciting has been a major theme throughout. The appearance of Leslie and Sarah ends whatever it is that is dull.

To the appearance of these sea monsters, Charlie and Nancy have different reactions. Charlie is petrified, and demands (reminiscent of the bee-mud incident) that Nancy find a stick so that he can fight them. By contrast, Nancy, although somewhat frightened, is fascinated by the monsters. She brings a small twig to Charlie, while Leslie lifts a huge branch; the implied sexual play, particularly the contrast of male potency, is quite funny. Believing that they are both going to die after Charlie is defeated in battle by Leslie, Charlie and Nancy hastily declare their love for each other.

At that moment, the airplane roars overhead for the third time in the act, and Leslie and Sarah become frightened and run away. Symbolically, the flight of the sea creatures serves to remind us how frighteningly far our modern technology has taken us from nature. For Nancy and Charlie, of course, the flight is hardly symbolic.

Nancy is awestruck by the entire happening. Although she has been frightened by the lizards, her sense of wonder and her exhilaration are greater and more compelling than her fear. In contrast, Charlie is relieved at the disappearance of the lizards and theorizes that their appearance was only a dream; he further conjectures that he and Nancy are dead, that they have succumbed to food poisoning from eating spoiled liver paste. Nancy answers:

> We may be dead already, Charlie, but I think we're going to die again. Here they come! (p. 51)

With the reappearance of the monsters, both Nancy and Charlie are truly frightened. Upon Nancy's suggestion, they both assume postures of animal submission and take on fixed smiles. Thus ends Act I.

In this first act, which is largely conversational, a middle-aged couple moves from a discussion of humdrum ways to escape loneliness, dullness, and emptiness to a confrontation with sea lizards, a wonderful, frightening fantasy.

Act II begins where Act I ended, as though the play were one long, uninterrupted act. The act division is useful, however, for the opening of the second act provides almost as great a surprise as did the appearance of the monsters: the monsters talk! At least for the moment, we have entered a world of pure fantasy.

However, the sense of absolute fantasy lasts only a short time. That the fantastic creatures are capable of speech makes them less fearsome and more humanoid. Always aware at some level that the creatures are make-believe, we nevertheless become involved, in fact deeply involved, in the interaction between the two couples and in what is being discussed. During this act, in the midst of a consideration of differences and concomitant bigotry, Leslie, the male lizard, says:

> Being different is . . . interesting; there's nothing implicitly inferior or superior about it. *Great* difference, of course, produces natural caution; and if the differences are too extreme . . . well, then, reality tends to fade away (p. 98).

Leslie's assertion is generally true. However, Albee has managed to maintain a keen sense of reality in us, despite the extreme differences between the lizards and the people, and between the world as depicted and the world of our quotidian existence. This is truly a remarkable achievement, not just a trick. The great chain of being (the human's direct link with the animal world) is a theme of the play, and Albee's powers of characterization, particularly his psychological insight and his great gifts of language, have enabled him to make a compelling portrayal of the monsters as early links in the chain. Through this linkage, Albee manages to bridge the gap between reality and unreality and to make our experience of each a means for a richer appreciation of the other.

More simply, just as Act I was essentially a dialogue between the two people, so Act II is a discussion between the two couples. As would be natural in a conversation, the pattern of couple-to-couple confrontation varies; each individual speaks to each other individual, and the partners sometimes address each other as a unit. The second act, like the first, is an extended conversation, interrupted periodically with a few instances of physical action.

The second act actually begins with an example of such action. Charlie and Nancy are still lying on their backs with feet in the air, the postures of submission they assumed at the end of Act I. Thus a comic bridge is extended from the first to the second act. After Leslie examines the humans, the couples speak apart. The lizards wonder what the humans are doing, and the humans then try to decide what to do in the face of this awful danger. On Nancy's urging, they decide to stay still and smile.

During this examination period we discover what is to be the keynote of the entire act. Leslie tells Sarah:

> Well . . . they don't look very . . . formidable—in the sense of prepossessing. Not young. They've got their teeth bared, but they don't look as though they're going to bite. Their hide is funny—feels soft (p. 57).

He then declares that they smell "strange." This scrutiny of the humans as a different and strange species continues throughout the act. As this becomes more intense, it deeply affects Nancy and Charlie and, as the examination is applied to the lizards, it affects them as well. In this way, Albee can ask what it means to be human and whether it is worthwhile trying to survive, the questions that link Act II to Act I. The principal mode for this examination, set forth right away, is that of contrast. Two sets of beings from different worlds, or in some measure, two sets of humans from different cultures, meet and compare notes.

After their initial scrutiny, the monsters decide to approach the humans together; Charlie is frightened but Nancy is somewhat fascinated. Comically, Leslie and Sarah argue, like husband and wife, over whether she should approach with him. This speech, with its expression of fear of the unknown and its familiar husband–wife role relations, makes the monsters seem real and tends to link the couples. The lizards speak to the humans and the humans respond, despite Charlie's hesitancy. They all say "hello" and exchange pleasantries.

When both sets of creatures declare that they do not intend to eat the other, the way is paved for more facile and substantial interaction. This specific discussion of intention leads Charlie to comment more generally on the eating habits of humans; he tries to explain, for example, that "we don't eat our own kind" (p. 66), but he is somewhat frustrated in making clear his meaning. This pattern of humans trying to explain rather fundamental things to nonhumans will continue throughout the play and will have the effect of exposing and confronting much of what it means to be human. On the subject of cannibalism, Leslie agrees:

Well, we don't eat our own kind, either. Most of us. Some (p. 66).

Such remarks (here and elsewhere) indicate the closeness of the human species to the animal world and subtly imply the unpleasant deviations of some human beings from civilized behavior.

The human explanation moves from eating habits to an attempt to explain handshaking, which brings some funny moments. Nancy and Sarah seem to interact more smoothly than Charlie and Leslie; Charlie is driven nearly mad when he tries to explain to Leslie why humans differentiate between "arms" and "legs" while animals have merely "legs." Despite the conversational tensions, they all ultimately shake hands, and this ritual seems to bring the couples a step closer. We feel that the development of real friendship is possible.

From handshaking, they begin to consider what frightens them; this discussion is motivated by a desire to avoid panic and consequent belligerence if one of them should happen to become frightened. They all agree that they are frightened by the unknown. For example, Charlie answers:

What frightens me? Oh . . . deep space? Mortality? Nancy . . . not being with me? (p. 73)

Then, on a lighter note, the humans try to explain what clothes are and why they wear them; Nancy defines the need as "to keep warm; to look pretty; to be decent" (p. 74). It is the attempt to explain *decency* (exposing the ridiculous puritanism of humans in the area of sex) that leads to a hilarious exploration—to Charlie's chagrin—of Nancy's breasts. Sarah's definitive analogy of Nancy's breasts to whale mammaries is both funny and serious; its funny side is the image of size with which Nancy's breasts are being associated. Its serious side is the linkage again of humans with other, supposedly lower, species.

When the couples begin to discuss pregnancy and birth, the apparently minor gap between animals and humans grows wider. While lizards lay eggs, humans do not. While lizards spawn hundreds of eggs at a time—Sarah estimates that she has laid seven thousand eggs—Nancy explains that humans give birth to one or two babies at a time. Sarah reveals that her eggs are carried for only a few weeks, while Nancy tells of the nine-month gestation period. Their subsequent discussion of child rearing also reveals radical differences. While Sarah's children merely float away, Nancy indicates that human children are kept at home for twenty years or so until they can care for themselves.

While this comparison has both its comic and educational facets, it actually leads into a rather serious area, one of vital concern to Albee in this play. In explaining "another reason" why humans keep their children with them, Nancy says "we *love* them" (p. 86). When the lizards inquire what *love* means, Nancy responds that it is "one of the *emotions*" (p. 87), which leads Sarah to ask for a definition of *emotions*; this definition is one of Charlie and Nancy's most difficult tasks. Although they cannot easily explain the emotions, especially love, it is Albee's notion that the human capacity for love and the range of emotional life are what separate humans from other animals. Later Charlie will make Sarah cry as he asks her to contemplate Leslie's ultimate departure through death. He will then explain that her reaction is an *emotional* response. It is Albee's notion that lower forms of life possess rudimentary emotional mechanisms, and that animals may not be as distant from us as we would wish to think.

Since this first attempt to explain the emotions fails, however, the couples discuss courtship and sex. This transition to lighter subject matter provides a relief and again emphasizes the similarity between humans and supposedly lower species. For example, when Sarah describes how males chased her and fought over her when she reached maturity, and when Leslie tells that he was attracted because she smelled good, we immediately recognize an analogy to the sensory components of human attraction and we realize how near we humans are to the world of the animals. This discussion of sex gets particularly funny when Nancy objects to Charlie's thinking Sarah may have had affairs.

Conversely, Charlie's assumption that human standards are inapplicable to the lizards nearly gets him into a fight with Leslie. He says that Leslie "has no grasp of conceptual matters, . . . hasn't heard of half the words in the English language, . . . lives on the bottom of the sea and has green scales" (p. 94). In fact, he suggests that Leslie is no more intelligent than a fish. This infuriates Leslie. Just as Charlie feels superior to Leslie, Leslie feels superior to fish; therefore, we perceive that both Charlie and Leslie are bigoted. But we also learn that Leslie is indeed capable of conceptualizing. It is he, in fact, who makes the observation that "*Great* difference . . . produces natural caution; and if the differences are too extreme . . . well, then, reality tends to fade away" (p. 98). In these lines, Albee once more lightly deflates human pride and pointedly reminds us of our link with the animal world.

Just at that moment, birds fly overhead and Nancy and Charlie try to explain what birds are. This discussion is intertwined with Sarah's description of how Leslie checks out conditions to make "sure a way is open for us . . ." (p. 99), and how he sets the parameters for their behavior. After Nancy says it is similar with humans, the discussion returns to birds, and Sarah likens their flying to the swimming of rays. Photography is also mentioned, but Charlie laughingly dismisses it as a topic, realizing it would be impossible to explain. They also laugh at how crazy everyone would think them were they to try to recount their interaction with the lizards.

This brings us back to Charlie's notion of the first act that they are dead, this time whimsically expressed by Nancy. She also returns to the first-act motif of Charlie's giving up versus her sense of wonder.

She explains that Charlie thinks they must be dead because he is a realist and a pragmatist and has rejected all sense of wonder on this earth (wonder being a matter for which Albee has subtly and ambiguously argued by presenting two fantastic beasts as symbols of believable wonder).

Leslie jumps right in on this life–death/reality–illusion question, and both couples are drawn into the ultimately unanswerable question of the reality of existence. When Charlie mentions Descartes' proposition, "I think: therefore I am," the prospect of having to define *thinking* for Leslie overwhelms him. In fact, everything all at once seems to overwhelm him, and he starts to crumble, saying, "Death is a release, if you've lived all right, and *I* have" (p. 109). Nancy wins him back to the world of the living by inserting her tongue into his mouth and giving him a long, lovely, French kiss. She explains that Charlie is all right; it is just that he has gone through life and found it a bit overwhelming.

Once again, intensity is interrupted by the roar of a jet plane overhead, the fifth time in the play and the second in Act II. Once more Nancy says, "Such *noise* they make," and Charlie ritually answers, "They'll crash into the dunes one day" (p. 111). Meanwhile, Leslie and Sarah have again run off in fear. Noticing their fear, Nancy and Charlie seem keenly sympathetic. Perhaps Charlie's recent confrontation with his own vulnerability, brought about by the lizards' questions, makes him especially sensitive to their plight. After the roar dies down, the couples come together once more. Charlie explains that planes are machines and, to Leslie's dismay, reveals that humans even have machines that go underwater.

Such a reference leads Nancy to mention Charlie's boyhood habit of submerging himself. Charlie is reluctant to discuss it and angrily asks the creatures why they came up on earth. Under stress, they reveal that they had lost a sense of belonging, of being comfortable down there. Here Albee is showing how dissatisfaction is a cause of change and development and how thoroughly grounded our human experience is in the life of the sea. Charlie is heartbroken as he considers the transition from simple, beautiful sea life to so-called higher forms of being.

Charlie proceeds to explain that humans also came from the sea and this naturally leads to an explanation of the theory of evolution. Charlie finally tells them that the key point for him was when some creature "poked his head out of the muck" and decided to stay on earth; "he split apart and evolved and became tigers and gazelles and porcupines and Nancy here . . ." (p. 124). Charlie also points out that some creatures went under and "turned into porpoises and sharks, and manta rays, and whales . . . and you" (p. 124). Sarah asks if this development, this "progress," is constructive. Charlie is unable to re-spond, but Nancy assures everyone that it *is* constructive, "because I couldn't bear to think of it otherwise" (p. 125).

Nancy goes on to explain that she values tools, art, and an awareness of mortality, and the discussion deepens. Charlie points out, rather harshly, that these things "separate *us* from the brute beast" (p. 126). He explains that the brute beast is "not even aware it's *alive*, much less that it's going to die" (p. 127). Here Albee is suggesting that this awareness, this crucial element of being a human instead of an animal, is also a source of human pain and perhaps of human ac-complishment. With an impulse that is at once jealous, vindictive, and loving, Charlie is struck with a need to make the lizards humanly aware of life, human emotions, and death. He says:

> . . . I'm impatient for you. I want you to experience the whole thing! The full sweep! Maybe I envy you . . . down *there*, free from it all; down there with the beasts? (p. 128)

He tries to encourage Sarah toward an awareness of death, but in so doing, he makes her cry and he makes Leslie intensely angry. Sarah wails:

> I want to go back; I don't want to stay here anymore. (*Wailing*) I want to go *back*! (*Trying to break away*) I want to go *back*! (p. 129)

This is one of the most striking moments of the play, as Albee sets forth the liability of being human, the deep sense of death and isolation that the human condition imposes.

Nancy, who has grown very close to Sarah, tries to comfort her. Charlie is very sorry for having caused her deep sorrow. Wildly angry, Leslie tries to choke Charlie to death for making Sarah cry. When Leslie states that "she's never done anything like that" (p. 130), Albee drives home his point that to have emotion, to cry, to learn about death, is to begin to be human. Nancy and Sarah exhort Leslie to stop choking Charlie, and finally he does, declaring that he and Sarah ought to return to the sea. The beasts resist Nancy's attempts to make them stay and, when Leslie touchingly puts out his paw to "shake hands," Charlie takes it. Nancy, in a final attempt to persuade them to stay, explains that although they may leave, they (i.e., the lower species) will have to come back some day. Then, as the confused lizards hesitate on top of the dune, Nancy and Charlie make the only meaningful effort that creatures can make to each other in the face of the void. They offer to help the lizards in their struggle to exist on this earth. Leslie, after descending a step down the dune and crouching, stands up straight and speaks the final line of the play: "All right. Begin" (p. 135). This is a highly affirmative conclusion to an essentially affirmative play, for Albee is suggesting that it is worthwhile to live upon this earth despite its troubles, its mysteries, and the imminence of death.

In *Seascape*, Albee has cast a broad, piercing light on the human condition. He has suggested that the human is but a step away from the simpler, lower animals, and that the simpler life—the life of the sea—is in many ways more attractive than life on this earth. The peace and beauty and mindless integration of the individual with nature is not to be found here. However, in the more complex human world, we have developed much that is artistically beautiful and technologically precise; such products have been the fruit of the developed human mind. More importantly, we have developed two principal capacities that distinguish us from animals: the ability to love and the awareness of death. The two capacities are interrelated, for human awareness of mortality draws us closer to our fellow creatures. Love, then, is our only weapon against the void.

Charlie and Nancy are in the process of confronting the void when we first encounter them in Act I. Basically, he wants to give up and rest; she wants to live actively. While we feel that Nancy's inclination is better because it is more in tune with human energy and natural optimism, Albee's purpose is not to tell us how to live. What he does show us, particularly in Act II, is that we are very deeply a part of—and a development from—the lower orders of nature (perhaps not comparatively so low after all). Therefore, we ought not to feel arrogant and emptily proud of our elevated station in the ongoing evolutionary process; rather, our part in the process should make us aware of our link with nature and give us a feeling of belonging to the world. But this feeling is not enough; to be human is to be separate, and this separateness is frightening. To confront this isolation, Albee contends, we have only human love. He demonstrates this by showing the great closeness of Nancy and Charlie in their most difficult moments, and the associated closeness of the humans for the lizards, from whom they do not wish to part at the conclusion.

Despite the heaviness and seriousness of Albee's concern, it is the catholicity of his vision and technique that really distinguishes this play. Albee shows himself open and sensitive to all facets of the human condition: the serious, the funny, the physical, the metaphysical, the actual, and the illusionary. All of his devices deserve commendation: his wit; the purity of his style, so maginificent in its captivation and alteration of normal speech; and his lizard fantasy, through which he reveals the human reality. The lizards are a bold theatrical stroke. Their appearance has dramatic power, and they serve, as does the isolated beach setting, to objectify the human condition and to bring us to a fundamental consideration of that condition; quite clearly, this is Albee's primary purpose.

Seascape is not only a remarkable aesthetic achievement, but it is also a highly affirmative statement on the human condition. Albee, an American writer, seems to have employed the techniques of the European playwrights Pinter and Beckett, and transformed them so that he could make a highly personal statement, one almost antithetical to their own. He seems to be saying that human life is worth living and that it is desirable to climb the evolutionary ladder in order to experience love, art, and the complexities of human interaction. It is desirable even if that means a certain loss of freedom, natural beauty, and the security possessed by the creatures of the sea. Albee has never made so affirmative a statement in his career; it is significant that *Seascape* should follow *All Over*, which dealt so heavily with death. With *Seascape*, Albee has, as if in a Lazarus-like rebirth of mind and spirit, magnificently affirmed life.

Entwining of the Strands

Of the five plays treated in this study, *Seascape* has the least intense atmosphere and relies the most on dialogue to move its action along.

Additionally, despite its crucial surrealistic dimension, it is second only to *Double Solitaire* in being the most realistic. Indeed, it is the confrontation of committed realism and outlandish surrealism, a primary Absurdist tool, that accounts for the play's considerable dramatic appeal and theatrical significance.

The play's realism lies in the human characters, whose speech, behavior, ethos, and situation clearly distinguish them as upper middle-class Americans. With their fortune made and their children grown, Charlie and Nancy are alone together on an extended vacation for the first time since they were married. They have come to a secluded beach—during the play they speak of seeing only a few other people farther down the beach—and we encounter them lolling and chatting in the afternoon sun, disturbed periodically by a passing airplane.

Since there is minimal action and much dialogue during most of the first act, the focus is firmly fixed on what Charlie and Nancy say to each other. Again, the conversation is essentially realistic, although the spareness of the dialogue, the couple's naturalistic objectification of life experience, and certain pronounced thematic strains indicate that their seemingly idle conversation is hardly the exercise in pure realism that it seems to be. Yet the overall manner and matter of the couple's conversation is decidedly realistic, and their relationship makes for easy identification. As is natural for a couple who have spent a life together, they talk about their mutual past and their hopes and plans for the future. In fact, much of their conversation during the first act focuses upon what plans, if any, they ought to make for their twilight years. Although Charlie seems to be content just to rest, Nancy wants a life of endless roaming and beachcombing—some excitement and vital involvements to insure and preserve their own vitality.

The couple speaks also of the family they have raised, of the pyramidal structure of that family, and of the children's probable astonishment at Nancy's notion of endless beachcombing. They speak also of Charlie's boyhood habit of enjoying submersion and of the present task of writing postcards even though it is boring. During all this conversation there is the verisimilitude of a familiar mutuality of concerns, believable dissatisfactions, easy camaraderie, interpersonal sensitivity, and serious and comic moments that characterize the behavior of a loving couple after long years of common struggle, common striving, and innumerable experiences deeply shared.

Among the most serious topics discussed by the couple, still ostensibly realistic in their manner, are the matters of aging and death. Both Charlie and Nancy are concerned with the passage of time and both indicate a desire to find tangible proof of the significance of the lives they have led. Clearly life is ongoing, but the determination of their particular imprint and/or raison d'être is frighteningly and amazingly elusive. In effect, their fear of old age and their effort to find an effective means to confront or elude it is the major motif of the first act. The couple finds no effective source of consolation, and the passage-of-time motif recurs like a refrain.

Although the talk of aging and death, with its concomitant objectification of life experience, falls within the realm of realistic dialogue, such discussion (and the fears it indicates and produces) creates tension and introduces strains of hopelessness and vulnerability. Such negativism is given further emphasis by the openness and vastness of the setting, the limitless and consequently frightening sea, surf, and sky. Such an environment serves to engender a cosmic loneliness in Charlie and Nancy, which gives their conversation a particular pungency. Moreover, the peace and quiet of the isolated beach is periodically violated by the roar of a passing airplane, which recurs throughout the play. This interruption not only is intrusive to Charlie and Nancy, but also seems to threaten them, if not all living creatures.

The motif of comfortable, passive escape versus active escape, the discussion of old age and death, the boundless setting, the spareness of the language, and the incursions by the airplane in themselves intensify the action until it reaches the very limits of realistic acceptability; what drives us clearly out of the domain of the purely realistic and into the nightmarish world of the Absurd is the surrealistic appearance, at the the end of Act I, of Leslie and Sarah, two great, green, humanoid sea lizards.

The theatrical shock at Act I's conclusion diminishes somewhat in Act II, when we learn that the lizards can communicate to the humans and do not intend harm. As the shock diminishes, the ensuing dialogue deepens our perception of realism versus surrealism; the conversation leads us to contemplate and explore the evolution of human life, the differences between human life and animal life, and, ultimately, the value amidst the pain of human life.

The essence of human life is subtly defined for us by Charlie and Nancy as they endeavor to explain various aspects of humanity to Leslie and Sarah. In a well-crafted, often comic series of comparisons and contrasts, Albee reveals both natural differences and ironic similarities between the two "species." Leslie and Sarah are husband and wife, and have a family, a history of biological attraction, a present mutual concern, a sense of pride, and a desire to learn and develop. The only real differences between the couples are in physical appearance; strength; the number of children each possesses; and the extent of technological, intellectual, and emotional development.

While the comparison produces much mirth and emphasizes and argues for a sense of wonder as one of the human being's greatest and most attractive capacities—the monsters become believable to us as well as to Charlie and Nancy—it also holds human life up to serious scrutiny. Furthermore, it produces a diminished sense of significance for Charlie and Nancy, inasmuch as they share so much with a lower species, and an even more trenchant sense that death and nothingness are a facet of both the human condition and the condition of all creatures. As with so many Absurdist plays, we do not know whether to laugh or cry as the amusing yet devastating interactional analysis between the couples proceeds.

Sarah, however, does know how to react; she begins to cry when Charlie explains to her what death is. This explanation and Sarah's reaction to it constitute the play's climax, and it then moves swiftly towards its essentially, if ambivalently, affirmative denouement. When Sarah learns that death involves permanent loss of or separation from Leslie, the lizards hastily decide to return to the sea. But the humans (especially Nancy) convince them to stay. Nancy explains that evolution will send their species back anyway and that she and Charlie could, and would like to, help them make the evolutionary transition. Enticed by the logic of Nancy's assertion and the offer of assistance, the monsters decide to stay.

While this conclusion makes *Seascape* the most positive of all the plays discussed in this study, it is not entirely winsome. Just as Charlie and Nancy have had to confront the ineluctable contingency of their lives and the sense that humans are simply an ingredient in universal flux, so Leslie and Sarah agree, by staying, to enter into a condition that they already know to be dangerous. All four know that life is essentially an experiment that carries a high probability of pain, that ultimately ends in death, and that carries no certainty whatsoever as to the benefits of "progress," the entire evolutionary thrust.

In the first act, Albee leads us to contemplate what the human couple should do with their old age. At the end of that act and the beginning of Act II, he leads us to speculate what the monsters will do to the couple. Soon, however, the theatrical sensationalism of the monsters' appearance passes, and the monsters themselves become a vital ingredient in the dominant questions of the entire play (articulated only partially in Act I): what are the contours and what is the meaning of life itself?

Inasmuch as the couples share a closeness, there is vitalist (i.e., experiential, whether or not logically defensible) affirmation in the play; and the hope for a progressive development in nature is also affirmative. However, neither the camaraderie of the characters nor the possibilities of future development hold any real answers for any of the individuals. They are caught in time with death, and its concomitants of loss and separation, as their dominant individual and communal future prospects. Therefore, while *Seascape* is not as bleak in tone as the plays of Rabe, Guare, and Bullins, it does share their perception (as does the Absurdist theatre in general) that life requires human beings to face the void. Moreover, *Seascape* possesses many Absurdist features, including the fusion of comic and tragic elements, a certain circularity of plotline (tangentially Absurdist), and, of course, the dreamlike, intermittently nightmarish atmosphere that is highlighted by the stunning presence of Sarah and Leslie. Except for the monsters' behavior, the Absurdist elements of *Seascape* are more subtly intertwined than they are in the works of Rabe, Guare, or Bullins. In fact, the distortions inherent in many of Albee's Absurdist elements are recognizable only through objective analysis. Absorption of the monsters into a realistic framework at once enhances the realistic and surrealistic dimensions of the play. In *Seascape*, the models of realism and Absurdism appear like two hovering presences, essentially distinct yet capable of intertwining, disengaging, and intertwining once more.

Seascape lacks a social protest dimension (except, perhaps, for a mild thrust at technology), and is clearly less realistic that Anderson's *Double Solitaire*, yet more realistic and, paradoxically, more fundamentally Absurdist than the works of Rabe, Guare, and Bullins.

Notes

[1]Harold Clurman, "Theatre," *The Nation*, 15 March 1975, p. 314.

[2]Mel Gussow, "Recalling Evolution of 'Seascape' Play, Albee Sees Tale Not of Lizard, but of Life," *The New York Times*, 21 January 1975, p. 40.

[3]Gussow, p. 40.

[4]T. E. Kalem, "Primordial Slime," *Time*, 10 February 1975, p. 57.

[5]Jack Kroll, "Leapin' Lizards," *Newsweek*, 10 February 1975, p. 75.

[6]Catharine Hughes, "Albee's *Seascape*," *America*, 22 February 1975, p. 136.

[7]Stanley Kauffmann, "*Seascape*," *The New Republic*, 22 February 1975, p. 22.

[8]Walter Kerr, "Albee's Unwritten Part," *The New York Times*, 2 February 1975, II, p. 5.

[9]Kalem, p. 57.

[10]Kroll, p. 75.

[11]Hughes, pp. 136–137.

[12]Kerr, p. 5.

[13]Brendan Gill, "Among the Dunes," *The New Yorker*, 3 February 1975, p. 75.

[14]Clive Barnes, "Albee's *Seascape* Is a Major Event," *The New York Times*, 27 January 1975, p. 20.

[15]Henry Hewes, "Albee Surfaces," *Saturday Review*, 8 March 1975, p. 40.

[16]Clurman, p. 314.

[17]"Albee: 'I Write to Unclutter My Mind,' " *The New York Times*, 26 January 1975, II, pp. 1, 7.

[18]Gussow, p. 40.

[19]Barnes, p. 20.

[20]Hewes, p. 40.

[21]Gill, p. 75.

[22]Clurman, p. 314.

[23]"Marginalia: Albee Cited for 'Seascape,' " *The New York Times*, 25 December 1975, p. 27.

[24]Edward Albee, *Seascape* (New York: Atheneum, 1975). All pages cited are from this edition.

The Strands Entwined

VII

$\mathcal{I}$n a *Commonweal* review of David Rabe's *Sticks and Bones*, Gerald Weales makes a comparison between that play and Arthur Miller's *All My Sons*. The superficial reason for the comparison is that both plays concern the return home from war of young American soldiers. Weales's comparison is worth quoting for it bears directly upon the thesis of this book that the entwining of the strands of realism and Absurdism allows current American drama to mirror so expressively the ethos of its culture:

> *Sticks and Bones* may be for the early 1970's what *All My Sons* was for the late 1940's—a play which, for all its imperfections, speaks directly and movingly to its own time. Rabe's play like Arthur Miller's, tells the story of a young man home from the wars, come to cleanse the imperfections in his family and the society which they represent. Yet, it is the differences between the two plays that explain the immediacy of *Sticks and Bones*. Miller's hero returns from a just war and brings with him a sense of brotherhood, of idealism intact; Rabe's hero comes back from a pointless and cruel war, half hoping that he can make his family look below the surface of their lives, and there is a touch of malevolence in the role he assumes. Miller's hero returns a whole man and finds the love of an understanding woman; Rabe's hero comes back blinded, having left behind the Vietnamese woman who taught him, in love, about the humanity of the others, those different from ourselves. Miller's hero sacrifices his father, in pain, for the hope of a better, cleaner world; Rabe's hero is sacrificed by his family to escape the pain of questioning the artificiality on which they thrive.
>
> Add that Miller's play is Ibsenite realism and that Rabe's is satiric, symbolic, poetic, an amalgam of most of the less excitable nonrealistic forms going around.[1]

In Weales's formulation, the world of Rabe's play is far more chaotic than that of Miller's. The reasons for going to war, the hero's psychological state and value structure, the home situation, and the shared assumptions of characters possess a certain clarity and stability in Miller's play that is lacking in Rabe's. Instead, in Rabe's play there is something rotten in the state of Vietnam/America, *but we are never entirely sure what the corruption is.* There is also a malevolence in Rabe's hero, which Miller's Chris (Christ?) does not have. The love of Anne is an option for Chris; in contrast, the object of David's love (Zung) has been destroyed before the play begins. In the killing of Joe Keller (killer?) there is a certain *justice* in the Miller play; in the killing of David by his family there is an even more powerful, symbolic reflection of *injustice* in a society and a world out of order. Indeed, the pop-art Nelson stereotype; the intermixture of the zany and the tragic; the attempted blending of familiar speech and quasi-poetic prose; the photographic and cinematic episodes; the interweaving of the apparition of Zung; and the entire panoply of naturalistic and nonnaturalistic details and events project a sense of disorder that is fundamentally alien to the familiar, understandable environment of Miller's *All My Sons.*

Although it differs greatly from *All My Sons,* Rabe's play is not an anomaly when compared to the plays of its own era; to a greater or lesser extent, images of chaos inform all five models of current American drama discussed in this study. Even more chaotic than *Sticks and Bones* are the characters and the situation portrayed in *The House of Blue Leaves,* and Guare's techniques are an equally rich mélange of diverse and multifaceted dramaturgy. The characters epitomize chaos: Bananas, who moves with doglike antics, who cooks Brillo pads instead of hamburgers, who is constantly disheveled, and who believes she cannot see the Pope because her fingernails are uneven; Bunny, who refuses to cook for a man unless he marries her, who has held a million jobs, who lives by innumerable trite slogans, and who flits from man to man; Corrinna, the glamorous movie star who is stone deaf; Billy, who makes such a third-rate picture as *Kangaroo;* Ronnie, who wants to become famous by blowing up the Pope; the three nuns, who like peanut butter and imported beer and who seem motivated solely by self-interest; and, finally, Artie, who feverishly writes and performs terribly trite songs, who guiltily fluctuates between love and hatred for Bananas, who desperately looks to Billy for his "big chance" for fame, and who ultimately murders his wife in an ironic gesture of love. Surely, to describe a world of such characters as chaotic is to describe it euphemistically. Guare presents this world through many experimental devices, including a mixture of hilarity and anguish, an audience address at the beginning of the play, vaudevillian stage action, an unexpected explosion, juxtaposition of subtle poetry (the blue leaves description) and a wild scramble by Ronnie and the nuns for the tickets to see the Pope, an interweaving of song and discussion, and an unlikely and ironic simile of religion and show business. The resultant madness creates a sense that the "zoo" is America or perhaps the earth itself, rather than simply the place where Artie works. Such a perception must surely give one pause if one believes, as I do, that what Guare intends to project is his own personal vision of life in this country and, perhaps, on this earth. To be in Guare's world is to be whirling out of control on a frightening and treacherous, albeit hilarious, amusement park ride with no one available to pull the switch in order to stop the machine.

Although the focus of Ed Bullins' play, American racial relations, is more circumscribed than that of the plays of Rabe or Guare, *The Taking of Miss Janie* is nonetheless equally chaotic and equally indicative of a world out of order. This is made trenchantly obvious by the failure of whites and blacks to work out a modus vivendi, and by the dominant characteristics of all characters—white and black: their exhaustion and suffering, their lack of clear values and shared assumptions, their distrust, their anger, their confusion, their violence, and their ultimate fragmentation and isolation. The situational chaos of *Miss Janie* is compounded by the gyroscopic movement of the play. Bullins employs abrupt temporal switches that take the action in and out of the present, past, and future; he mixes naturalistic and fantastic elements; he juxtaposes monologue and dialogue; he breaks dramatic conventions, including that of aesthetic distance; and he uses lighting and stylized movement freely. The text is sometimes contradictory and the symbolism inconclusive, even in regard to Miss Janie herself. The characters sometimes speak seerlike predictions, and the dialogue often contains vituperative propaganda and elements of violence and hatred; racial and religious pejoratives are used freely.

Bullins' own rage and prejudices flavor the dialogue and action, which includes a rape—violent, brutal, and shocking in its impact on Janie, who believed in Monty's friendship; a party, throughout which the atmosphere is relentlessly tense and charged; and a bleak and terrible conclusion, which suggests the destruction of both a personal bond between Monty and Janie and, symbolically, a bond between all blacks and whites in America. All of these elements help to create a kind of pandemonium, a hellish, unstructured, unsafe world in which people lose all sense of interpersonal solidarity and live in isolation from each other, making true contact, if at all, not through love, but through aggression.

Although the naturalism of Robert Anderson's *Double Solitaire* might encourage us to view the work as Milleresque, a brief scrutiny of its content and structure indicates that it is quite different from the plays of Arthur Miller. Central to *Double Solitaire* is the relationship of a middle-aged couple, Charley and Barbara; we learn quite early that the marital condition is hardly agreeable to either party. A loss of excitement, solidarity, and profound communication has drawn them apart. When they are asked to reaffirm their marriage vows, Charley becomes panicky because he is forced to realize that there is no longer a spark or real substance in the marriage; Barbara, sexually frustrated, disillusioned, and exhausted, reveals that she too regards their situation as empty and unfulfilling. Charley's parents, who have asked the couple to reaffirm their vows, have themselves been living a lie. The mother is put off by the father's indelicate ways, and the father is deeply alienated from his wife because she has no interest in maintaining the sexual aspect of their relationship. Also, they have little intellectual or emotional rapport. Mr. Potter, Charley's father, urges Charley to adjust; in fact, he warns that the isolation may deepen with time. Mrs. Potter tells Barbara that married people must find grounds for staying together rather than grounds for divorce. She suggests shared, safe diversions; for example, she and Mr. Potter play double solitaire together; the play's title becomes a powerful image of their isolated, separated, lonely lives and the mundane contrivances that replace honest joy in an aging marriage. Although they plan to show slides of their wedding at their fiftieth anniversary, those slides, frozen images of happier times, will represent only romantic memories, not current reality. Charley's son Peter, although unmarried and very much in love, also employs photography to project the meaning of his relationship; his film is also, from the play's perspective, a distortion of truth. In the film, Peter happily rushes home from work to join Melinda in a passionate bath scene. The excessive romanticism of the film; Peter's naive declaration that they will stay together as long as their love survives; and the image of inexorable temporal movement from youth to middle to old age, as evidenced by the condition of his parents and grandparents, all foreshadow pain and disillusionment. Inevitably, he will experience what he now scorns. Present bliss will in time become only a memory as the winter of age replaces the summer of youth.

Charley and Barbara's friends also provide little solace. Sylvia, having divorced her husband, prefers to remain a "visitor" in the lives of many men. Avoiding any lengthy commitment that might become a tiring habit rather than a spontaneous, vital tryst, Sylvia acknowledges that she has given up long-range security in favor of current excitement. Ultimately, she will be lonely; already, she is lonely on holidays and other " tribal times," when her male guests return to their wives. But marriage has never been good to her. Marriage has also not been satisfying for Charley's friend George, but he has stayed married, kept up appearances, and depended on extramarital affairs. He urges Charley to follow suit. Although Charley cannot do this, he admits that he has contemplated an affair with Maria, a writer whose work he has edited. From Charley's conversation with George, there emerges the most frightening notion of the play. George says that "marriage is a transitional institution" and that people are currently caught within the transition.

Although marriage will fade, there is presently nothing to replace it. Therefore, when Charley tries to reactivate Barbara's earlier passion by taking her to a secluded beach, we realize that, even if their relationship were recemented, the marital state is hardly a dependable buffer against personal emptiness and life's dissatisfactions. That Charley regards physical sex as the deepest link between them suggests that the attachments of human beings, even married human beings, are far from solid. Although she knows that they will fail, Barbara agrees, upon Charley's insistence, to try once more to recapture their earlier passion, even though many years have passed. Superficially, this resolve seems an optimistic conclusion to the play. However, we can hardly be sanguine about their marriage specifically, or about all marriages in general, if we accept Anderson's vision of hopeless isolation.

Were the content of *Double Solitaire* insufficient to unsettle us, its structure powerfully supports and mirrors its vision of isolation and assures that the chaotic condition of the characters is vividly brought home to us. Clive Barnes has ambiguously referred to *Double Solitaire* as both a "well-made" play and a play of "strange" structure. If by "well-made" Barnes means simply that the play is appropriately crafted, he is right. As a writer of plays, movies, and radio scripts for many years, and as a teacher of other playwrights, Anderson does know quite well how to put together a play skillfully, and has done so here. If, however, Barnes means to suggest, as indicated earlier, that this is a "well-made play" in the more formal and literary sense of that term, then he is patently wrong. The term "well-made play" was coined by the French playwright Scribe to describe the major tradition of Western drama of the latter half of the nineteenth century. As a convention, it signifies that a play contains an essentially logical structure, unwavering cause and effect relationships, resolutions to conflicts, and strong climaxes (at the end of each act, as well as of the play) toward which the action builds throughout.[2]

This definition hardly describes *Double Solitaire*. The bare stage, symmetrically set with husband and wife separated; the episodic structure; the deliberate exclusion of precise time or place delineation; the monologues; the panoramic consideration of many characters and their lives; the absence of foreshadowing and mechanistic plot development; the unexpected emphasis on Barbara's outlook in the last scene; and the essential irresolution of conflict and absence of a strong climax at the conclusion all serve to exclude *Double Solitaire* from the "well-made" rubric. Moreover, there are no twisted incidents, no secret letters, no delayed messengers (all frequently encountered contrivances of the "well-made play") to mar the fluidity, grace, and breadth of the work. The "well-made play" assumes a certain rational order in life and transmits that assumption into an essentially rationalistic art form.

Because of *Double Solitaire*'s orderly presentation of subject matter, dialogue, and characterization, we may get the impression that a comforting rationalism informs the work. Closer scrutiny indicates, however, that fragmentation, isolation, and instability characterize the lives of the characters, their marriages, and perhaps life itself.

Like *Double Solitaire*, Edward Albee's *Seascape* has sophisticated conversation; believable, reasonable characters; and a superficially familiar situation: a middle-aged married couple searching for meaning. Such elements may seem to belong to a more orderly, more confident brand of dramaturgy, reflective of a rationalistic life view. But this is not so. A more careful examination will reveal that the chaos is there. The very subject of the play is unsettling, as is the setting.

In the first act, we join the main characters, Nancy and Charlie, who are off alone on a vacation. Their children have grown up, their economic future is secure, but their lives feel empty. Not only is the excitement gone from their marriage, but time itself seems hostile in a world where all meaning has been lost. Nancy wants to regain some of life's excitement, although her suggestion for doing so (beachcombing) seems escapist; in contrast, Charlie simply wants to bury his weary head in the sand, to rest after a long life. The setting for the exchange of these views is a sunny, isolated beach. No other people are in view, and the couple seems somehow alien from the land, sea, and sky. They are interrupted only by the drone of a passing plane, which annoys them and seems menacing.

In both this first act and the second act (in which Charlie and Nancy interact with the sea lizards), the familiar behaviors of life, as well as its history and prospects, are held up to objective scrutiny. The language itself, so carefully sculpted by Albee, so malleable and yet so suggestive and explosive, serves only to increase the uncertainties already produced by the discussion. Everything seems so tentative; humanity seems so clearly and unflatteringly a product of the evolutionary process; and death, so imminent a threat and so repeatedly discussed, obviously closes all. Indeed, the unexpected entrance of the sea creatures—their awesome physical appearance, their capacity to speak and to conceptualize, and their introduction by Albee into the dramatic fabric of the play and the life fabric of Charlie and Nancy—is but the crowning stroke in an anxiety-producing conception of the vulnerability and fragility of human life.

In a *New York Times* interview with Mel Gussow, Albee states that *Seascape* is "a true-to-life story." He goes on to explain:

> The events could actually happen. There are still prehistoric fish at the bottom
> of the ocean. It's conceivable that they could evolve. In the course of the play,
> the evolutionary pattern is speeded up billions of revolutions.[3]

It is not only Albee's imposition of the sea monster fantasy that sets us awry; his passionately serious egalitarian attitude toward his fantasy, grounded obviously in serious belief, makes it even more upsetting than comical. What is true? What is stable? We must ask and re-ask ourselves such fundamental questions as we witness fantastic sea creatures entering an essentially naturalistic, familiar world. What is true or stable if we are not even certain that the incredible fantasy is fantastic, that the wild fiction is actually fictional?

Chaos, therefore, is a primary characteristic of the plays considered in this study, high quality plays that are indicative of the current state of our drama. It appears not only as a primary ingredient of the action and dialogue, but also as a strong motivating force in the very conception of these works. This emphasis on chaos differentiates the plays sharply from *All My Sons* (and from a whole range of dramatic works analogous to *All My Sons*) that were produced in America only two decades before. The chaos is represented by a dwelling upon fragmentation, a repeated evocation of a valueless world, a wholesale mixing of genres, and a presentation of a very dark side of human character; the reasons for such emphasis on chaos are difficult to assess. My guess is that Vietnam had much to do with it, as did our growing awareness of the Third World and its problems, new developments in genetic research, the sexual revolution, the increasing urban problems, and the information explosion brought about by computer technology and the expansion of mass media coverage of international events. Surely, the awareness of chaos, of the bleak, dark side of human existence, was part and parcel of modern European philosophy, but until relatively recently Americans had been sheltered from or buffered against such truths. Then, as the 1960s came to a close, the European awareness infected or invaded, infested or entered (depending upon one's outlook) the American consciousness. Even for Americans, the world had become complex and uncertain.

Were we to search for a literary or dramatic analogue to this new, important strain in American drama, we would surely find it quite easily. It exists in what is called the Theatre of the Absurd. While an awareness of chaos is significant in our drama, it is the central, crucial, underlying, and informing vision of this European expression. Essentially a post–World War I phenomenon, a response to that war and to various earlier strains in European thought, Absurdism was foreshadowed in the Dadaist movement of the 1920s, and as early as the 1890s with Alfred Jarry. It reached its culmination in the 1940s in works by such writers as Beckett, Ionesco, Genet, and Adamov, and, later, in the works of such English playwrights as Pinter and Simpson.

In 1961, in an extraordinary work of theatre criticism entitled *The Theatre of the Absurd*, Martin Esslin traced the history and elucidated the characteristics of the Absurdist movement. Unlike its contemporary, the Existentialist Theatre, which also responded to our awareness of chaos, the Theatre of the Absurd sought to bring form and subject matter into harmony; according to Esslin, rather than arguing convincingly and rationally about absurdity, this movement sought to present that absurdity in the very body and movement of its plays. In order to do so, it de-emphasized and devalued language and substituted mime; it rejected the unity and consistency of character; and it created a nightmarish, fantastic experience on the stage in preference to the familiar and popular naturalistic mode. Finally, it confronted and presented the bleak side of human existence expressed in Absurdist and Existentialist philosophy; at the same time, it took an objective and calm look at human behavior and presented a highly comic view of the human *antihero*, which seemed much truer and more responsive to the actualities of modern experience than the vestigial *heroic* outlook that had lingered on and become an outdated tradition in European literature. In the Theatre of the Absurd, the playwright's aim became psychological truth rather than some artificially contrived story or statement, however ideologically or poetically appealing. By fusing form and content and by dispensing with false symmetry and mechanical effects as well as a host of artificially imposed, traditionally valued assumptions characteristic of conventional drama, the Theatre of the Absurd spoke to the modern consciousness as the earlier drama could not.

Esslin's description of Absurdist drama might also be applied, in differing degrees, to the plays included in our study. In fact, Weales suggests that *Sticks and Bones*, if not a direct example of Absurdist theatre, is yet ripe for valuable discussion in Esslin's terms. The pointlessness of war's cruelty takes us a long way toward a conception of the meaninglessness of life; the maimed, blinded hero shares much in common with the often maimed antiheroes of the Absurdist world (e.g., Ham, the blinded postholocaust antihero of Beckett's *Endgame*); and the hero's assumption of a role hardly recognizable to his family protrays in some measure the Absurdists' frequent rejection of character consistency. Finally, the following elements, all cited by Weales, suggest further analogies to Absurdist theatre: the absence of love and order, the breakdown of values, and the free-wheeling mélange of genres that allows comic and noncomic elements to exist side by side. As with the Theatre of the Absurd, *Sticks and Bones* often carries us imaginatively beyond the world of familiar conscious experience. With its superstructure of familiar and realistic detail that has been reorganized, truncated, expanded, and changed in emphasis, *Sticks and Bones* often has the quality of an Absurdist nightmare. Additionally, its comic surface and bleak life view are certainly reminiscent of, if not directly analogous to, the texture of the works of Beckett and Ionesco.

A similar claim might be made for Guare's anguished, yet highly theatrical and wildly funny, treatment of disillusionment in *The House of Blue Leaves*. Similarly, Bullins' hellish, raging, racial war, *The Taking of Miss Janie*, possesses the quality of phantasmagoria and ends in seemingly preordained violence, the rape and its subtle accompanying violence of the death of Miss Janie's spirit and the loss of human connection. The primary image of Albee's *Seascape*, the startling appearance and integration of fantastic sea monsters, possesses the quality of dream, if not of nightmare. Finally, Anderson's *Double Solitaire*, admittedly the most conventional of these plays, exhibits the breakdown of values, the flux of personality, the intermixture of comic and serious concerns, and the very lonely and tentative condition of its main characters, Charley and Barbara, who sit like two lost souls on an empty beach. There is a certain bleak inevitability suggested by the similar conflicts of desired ideal versus unfulfilling actuality in each generation of Potters, and Anderson's use of bare stage and shadows, his episodic structure, his obvious elimination of precise references to time and locale, and his extensive employment of photography to mirror and expand thought and imagination convey a general quality of dream. However much *Double Solitaire* shares with naturalistic theatre, its theatrical experimentalism and its life view are influenced greatly by the Absurdist mode as well.

Four of the five plays in this study, then, contain definite strains of Absurdist theatre; the fifth play, *Double Solitaire*, although essentially naturalistic, still exhibits the influence of Absurdist theatre. This trend toward Absurdism, however, should not be misconstrued as an indication that current American drama belongs to the Theatre of the Absurd; rather, it is my belief that the Absurdist mode should be considered a principal influence, in fact one of the *two* principal influences, upon the focus and structure of current American drama.

The other principal influence had its impact on American drama earlier than Absurdism. Gerald Weales aptly alluded to it when he described Miller's *All My Sons*, in the *Commonweal* article previously cited, as "Ibsenite realism." Such a term is particularly applicable to a Miller play because Miller, more than any other American playwright, has been influenced by Ibsen, the father of modern drama. Allowing, of course, for the differences in time and nationality, Miller faithfully reproduces much of Ibsen's liberalism, his reverence for loving family relationships, his use of the "well-made play" structure with its suggestion of the flashback, his psychological realism, his political and social outlook, and his blending of social and existential concerns. Miller further demonstrated his philosophical alliance with Ibsen by writing an adaptation of Ibsen's *An Enemy of the People*.

What Miller achieved in pure and faithful manner was attempted, in somewhat less faithful form, by most of the major modern American playwrights. Although Eugene O'Neill, Elmer Rice, and Maxwell Anderson obviously show the influences of European poetic drama and (particularly German) expressionism and of the surrealism of Absurdist drama's precursors, still the major ingredient, the dominant mode in the work of all these playwrights, is Ibsenite realism.

Interestingly, when Esslin wrote his monumental study of Absurd-ist drama, he cited Edward Albee as the only bona fide American Ab-surdist. He rejected Robert Hivnor's *Too Many Thumbs* as too op-timistic, despite its superficial similarity to Ionesco's plays; he also re-jected Jack Gelber's *The Connection* because it vacillates between Ab-surdism and the realism of social reform. However, Esslin praised Albee's *The Zoo Story* as "akin to the work of Harold Pinter," and he praised *The American Dream* as "a play that clearly takes up the style and subject matter of the Theatre of the Absurd and translates it into a genuine American idiom" and "a promising and brilliant first example of an American contribution to the Theatre of the Absurd."[4] As evidence of *The American Dream*'s place in Absurdist theatre, Esslin specifically cites Albee's attacks on the ideals of progress, optimism, and faith; his mockery of the American middle class; his exposure of the "disagreeable verities" beneath the façade of American business; and his masterful "combining of clichés."

Whether Esslin would admit subsequent Albee plays into the Ab-surdist canon we do not know. It is doubtful, and Esslin's phrase, "and translates it into a genuine American idiom," takes on a particular force in this context. I am afraid that much is lost—or gained—in at-tempts at such translation into American idiom; few American plays, including Albee's subsequent works, would fit neatly and absolutely into the rather precise territory delimited by Esslin. The point, however, is that *The American Dream* was the first American Absurd-ist play, that Albee's subsequent works partake profoundly of this mode, and that he is among the most significant American playwrights since Eugene O'Neill. Moreover, during the last decade, more and more American plays have integrated the vision and employed the theatrical techniques of the Theatre of the Absurd.

In 1968 Bernard F. Dukore wrote an article entitled "Off Broad-way and the New Realism," in which he suggested that the 1960s brought America a new breed of playwrights whose works did not fit into conventional categories. He listed Jack Gelber, Ken Brown, and Leroi Jones as among the best of the new breed, citing Gelber's *The Connection*, Brown's *The Brig*, and Jones's *The Dutchman* as deserving of special commendation. He claimed that what characterized these plays and differentiated them from works of traditional realism was their employment of so many nonrealistic techniques to convey their essentially realistic, actually naturalistic, observations. For this reason, he said that these plays belonged to a new dramatic category, the "New Realism," and that these playwrights might well be carving out a new path for American drama.[5]

In the same article, he suggests that all three playwrights are indebted to the shock-oriented theatrical philosophy of Antonin Artaud. As Dukore states, "All three plays blend an attack on the values of the audience with an attack on its senses and emotions in order to create a direct theatrical experience."[6] Dukore was essentially correct in calling attention to the worth of these plays; they are among the best of the 1960s. He was also correct in noting that they engage in social criticism, assault the senses, and blend realistic and nonrealistic strains. However, he was was wrong in his ultimate judgment of their influence. His error was most tellingly conveyed in the last paragraph of his article, where, in partial correctness, he differentiates these works from those of the Absurdist school and then praises the writers for their lack of interest in the Absurdist mode. He contends that the concept of the absurdities of life has become a cliché and suggests that the merit and truth of the new school is that its writers respond "to the cruelty of existence as they see it inside themselves and as they find it reflected in the world around them at a particular moment in history."[7]

Quite accurately, Dukore claims that these works are not Absurdist in mode, but his disclaimer must be qualified. By employing Dukore's own description of the nonrealistic facets of these plays, we can readily see how much they are influenced by Absurdist theatre. Citing the rejection of conventional dramaturgy as typical of these plays, Dukore calls attention to the de-emphasis on plotting and "the use of a cycle to suggest recurrence and deadly inevitability."[8] Cyclical structure and de-emphasis on the linear plot are, of course, familiar Absurdist techniques, as are the nightmarish qualities to which he calls attention in all of the plays; furthermore, the metaphor of waiting employed in *The Connection* obviously owes much to Beckett's Absurdist *Waiting for Godot* or, at least, to the ethos that produced that work. Even in his citing of Artaud's influence, Dukore leads directly to the Absurdists, whose dramaturgy certainly owes much to Artaud's philosophy and practice.

It is clear, then, that these plays of "New Realism" are, in fact, greatly influenced by Absurdist theatre; however, they also resist that influence, as Dukore suggests. It is that resistance, that failure to integrate the Absurdist vision, that ultimately accounts for the deficiencies of these works and of Dukore's claim that they foreshadow a major new direction in American drama. In contrast to Dukore, I prefer to look upon these plays as intermediate, experimental stages on the path toward such integration. Either way, as non-Absurdist works or as incipient Absurdist works, they fail to mirror substantially and profoundly the American ethos of their day. Drugs, racial tensions, and military brutality are, regrettably, segments of the American ethos, but a broader, more nihilistic, existential awareness has crept into our consciousness.

When we reflect that *The Connection* and *The Brig* were both originally produced by Malina and Beck's Living Theatre, we have a key both to their orientation and to their ultimate deficiency. While the Living Theatre was an exciting experiment of the 1960s (like Chaikin's Open Theatre, Jerzy Grotowski's nonverbal theatre, and Charles Marowitz's Open Space Theatre in London), its essentially nonverbal emphasis ultimately proved itself unable to speak to our deepest needs as modern human beings. It is for these reasons that the works of all of these artists stand as historically interesting experiments, but finally unfulfilling artistic expressions.

In essence, *The Connection*, *The Brig*, and even *The Dutchman* belong to the ethos of the nonverbal shock theatre of the 1960s, the Theatre of Cruelty. As such, they substitute rhythm for thought and they rely on an assault of the senses rather than the more subtle approach of meaningful language. Surely, prior to these plays American theatre failed to involve the audience ritually; but these plays, like the experiments in nonverbal theatre of the 1960s, go too far in a single direction. Moreover, the essentially limited, socially grounded vision of these works of "New Realism" fails to take into account a profound change in awareness in America. Perhaps the strength of these plays is their limitation: because they are stark and brutal, they surprise and shock us. However, they fail to integrate that dark confrontation of meaninglessness that has also, alas, become a part of the American ethos—especially since our involvement in Vietnam. The so-called "New Realism," therefore, in its exclusion and consequent ultimate denial of Absurdist concerns, is terribly circumscribed and surely not the path that American drama is taking or ought to take. The better, if more dangerous, path is the path of fusion, an entwining of the strands of realism and Absurdism, the subject of this study.

Esslin rejects Gelber's *The Connection* from the Theatre of the Absurd and categorizes it as realist theatre of social reform because the play "culminates in a plea for reform of the drug laws"; he would have a more difficult task if he were to try to reject from Absurdism *The Taking of Miss Janie*, *The House of Blue Leaves*, or *Sticks and Bones* on similar grounds. Admittedly, there are social dimensions, and even vital strains of social criticism, in these works; however, in each case, the playwright's vision and ultimate purpose cannot be described in terms of social criticism. Bullins depicts the relationship of blacks and whites as an abyss of quasi-hopeless confusion. Guare's evocation of the tawdry, fraudulent American ethos is surely secondary to his bleak vision of the blighted quest for meaning by Artie Shaughnessy, who is driven to madness by the conditions of life, and who commits murder as an act of love. Similarly, the Ozzie and Harriet stereotype provides Rabe with a stimulating pop-art vehicle for his *secondary* aim, a censuring of the emptiness, ugliness, ethnocentricity, and materialism of American culture; his *primary* vision is projected through David, who pierces the American façade to demonstrate the anguish of many of our "solid citizens," the insubstantial quality of our family life and our institutions, the anguish of isolation, and the death of meaning and love. In the late moments of the play, as the family nonchalantly helps David to commit suicide (and the blood pours from his wrist), Ozzie says:

No, he's not gonna die, Rick. He's only gonna nearly die. Only nearly.[9]

Such euphemistic words convey Rabe's contempt for American self-delusion; although Rabe surely projects social criticism, the horror of the suicide/murder climaxes his terribly bleak pronouncement on all aspects of human sensitivity and the overall human condition.

The social protest is there—ambivalently—in Rabe's conclusion, as it is in the plays of Guare and Bullins. It exists—also ambivalently—even in the works of Ibsen and Miller, as a social/existential axis, a plea against social wrong and an awareness of the hopeless, meaningless state of humanity; paradoxically, Ibsen and Miller present both aspects side by side. The change is simply one of emphasis. Whereas the works of O'Neill, Miller, Williams, and Inge present human suffering, they do not wallow in it. There is in such works a controlled presentation—a carefully crafted orderliness of plot, a familiarity of language, an essentially serious atmosphere, and a clarity and simplicity that, in the works of Rabe, Guare and Bullins, has given way to a bitterness, a wildness, a wholesale mixing of genres, and a further dilution of American optimism.

The optimism is there, however, and the very ferocity of the social protest indicates a desire by the playwrights to change and better society; such a desire is lacking in the mainstream of European Absurdist theatre. Surely Ionesco parodies the stupidity and pomposity of the French bourgeoisie, but the social ridicule of the new American plays differs greatly from the social ridicule of such plays as *The Chairs*, *Jack or The Submission*, or *The Bald Soprano* (in which a married couple discover that since they live together and have the same names they must necessarily be husband and wife). The social ridicule in the European drama is always part of the Absurdist "argument," a step toward elucidating the bleak condition of human beings. If the effect is satiric, that effect is peripheral and secondary. By contrast, in the American plays the social ridicule and concomitant social protest are distinct from, albeit related to, the vision of the void. The American dramatists expend much creative energy exposing the deficiencies of our culture. If, as I contend, their passion for social justice is related to their existentialist vision, it might be argued that they see and present a logical relation between the two perspectives: human life, however bleak it is, is made more bearable when one kind of chaos (social injustice) is not introduced into the daily lives of individuals who must ultimately confront the chaos of existence itself (an injustice of even broader dimensions). This passion for rectification then creates an ambivalence—a rich and vital tension—in the works of American playwrights. Although our playwrights have become more confident in expressing a negativistic life view, an optimistic strain still exists within even our bleakest works.

This difference between our plays and the bona fide European Absurdist canon is not solely a matter of this strain of American optimism. There are other differences that deserve mention. Like the

European Absurdist plays, our best current works are short, episodic, bleak, nightmarish pieces—a hybrid of forms in which theatrical imagery is vital and character consistency is sometimes sacrificed. However, such a general observation must be qualified. In the plays we have discussed, naturalism is still a powerful ingredient; as such, it rarely allows a total loss of character consistency or a departure from cause and effect relationships to move the plot along. We must admit that these plays do have linear plots, however thin they may be. Although *Seascape* is essentially a discussion, Charlie and Nancy move toward, and ultimately achieve, a new view of life at the play's end. *Double Solitaire* exposes a pre-existent condition, but Charley contemplates his marriage and finally does try to revitalize it. *The House of Blue Leaves*, a hilarious, sometimes anarchic vaudevillian comedy of errors, presents a day in the life of Artie Shaughnessy, in which his futile dreams are destroyed. Even though the body of *The Taking of Miss Janie* hardly relates in a precise cause and effect relationship to the beginning and ending that frame it, the epilogue assault foreshadows, albeit retrospectively, the rape committed in the prologue. Finally, *Sticks and Bones* provides a sadomasochistic flailing at American culture; however, it begins with David's return home and ends with his family helping him to kill himself because of what occurs in the interim. Whereas the European Absurdist works lack plots and precise cause and effect relationships, the current American plays, while plotless in comparison to earlier American plays, are still quite accurately described as plotted plays.

The current American plays, although generally longer than those of the Absurdists, are still short; their brevity helps them to reflect, as Charles Marowitz says, the immediacy of current fragmented experience.[10] However, brevity may have adverse effects on plotting, and vice versa. For example, let us recall John Guare's comment on structure in his interview with Henry Hewes.[11] Guare had found that his anarchic, free-spirited attitude toward plotting had created limitations on his freedom of expression. Although his spontaneous method had enabled him to explore himself, it allowed him to write only short plays. As a result, he was determined to find a happier balance between personal concerns and the problems of structure, and he achieved this balance in the writing of *The House of Blue Leaves*. His development, I believe, is symptomatic of the experiments and time needed by American playwrights to incorporate the Absurdist methodology effectively.

Another difference between current American drama and the European Absurdist works has to do with language. The monologues and dialogues of the plays in this study show the influence of Absurdism. For example, our playwrights (particularly Albee and Guare) surrealistically intensify language, and they alter and highlight cliché, for which they possess a keen ear. However, naturalistic dialogue still plays a vital role in our drama. Although the nonverbal theatrical dimension of our plays has grown, language is still far more crucial in American drama than it is in the Absurdist canon. Rabe, Guare, and Bullins share the dramatic mainstream with such playwrights as Albee and even Anderson, whose writing clearly reveals that Ibsenite realism is still a powerful influence in American dramaturgy.

In this regard, a special word about Edward Albee's *Seascape* and his development as a dramatist is in order. Prior to *Seascape*, Edward Albee wrote *All Over*; as mentioned earlier, commentators wondered if the title and theme of this work signified that Albee's works were "all over." Because *All Over* was deeply concerned with death and reactions to death, some critics believed that Albee's underlying message was that he could find nothing more in life to stimulate him. As is true with the Absurdist writers, Albee's act of writing was itself a kind of life affirmation; however, little else affirmative can be found in *All Over*. Obviously it did not signify the end of his writing, though; and, as Albee explained, it was merely half of an earlier conception that included a consideration of life as well as of death. This consideration of life ultimately became *Seascape*. Its particular blend of optimism and subtle wit represents a new aspect of the Albee canon. Having described personal isolation in *The Zoo Story*, social isolation in *The Death of Bessie Smith*, intellectual isolation in *Who's Afraid of Virginia Woolf?*, religious isolation in *Tiny Alice*, communal isolation in *A Delicate Balance*, and existential isolation in *All Over*, Albee seemed rejuvenated. It was as if the man who had bombarded America's fraudulent institutions, loss of values, and colossal hypocrisy had somehow purged himself of fury, disillusionment, and despair and had come back, like Lazarus, to make an essentially affirmative statement about life. The affirmation is subtle, though, and it emerges from beneath Albee's characteristic barbs.

Seascape does ridicule our bigotry, selfish pride, and technological ugliness; it holds the human animal up to scorn and mockery; and it shows that isolation is a part of life, and that death, all too quick in coming, is an unknown terror. However, Albee's touch is light and his sympathy and empathy are very great in *Seascape*. Moreover, underneath the barbs lie very affirmative statements: that human love is beautiful, that life has wonders and prospects for us all if we will search, and that we all belong to a magnificent grand system of evolutionary development. In essence, then, Albee has confidently incorporated the negativistic outlook and spontaneous techniques of the Absurdists with the naturalistic mode of Ibsen, as translated into the optimistic American ethos. Albee thus epitomizes again a new spirit in our dramaturgy as he did fifteen years earlier, when he was hailed by Esslin as our first Absurdist playwright. At that time, Esslin said, "Edward Albee . . . comes into the category of The Theatre of the Absurd because his work attacks the very foundations of American optimism."[12] Today, we might suggest with equal accuracy that Albee has profoundly taken into account the negativistic vision of the Absurdists and has transcended that vision by incorporating it into a renewed faith in the beauty and meaning of life. The formal, technical properties of *Seascape*, as well as its conception and content, bespeak this magnificent fusion. Once more, Edward Albee may be described as a forerunner of what is to come in our drama.

Of Robert Anderson a comment is also in order. Anderson's projection of the exhaustion of a marriage seems Absurdist in its negativistic view of the institution of marriage itself, which is one of our few sources of strength against isolation and loss of life's meaning. However, despite its Absurdist qualities, *Double Solitaire* more nearly fits the classification of Ibsenite realism than it does the later Absurdist mode. That Anderson felt both of these influences made his writing truer and more comprehensive; that he, as an American playwright, decided to use both significant modes is truly exciting. His divergence from such younger playwrights as Guare, Rabe, and Bullins (and even, somewhat, from Albee) constitutes an advantage for American theatre. The dramatist's option to employ either or both of these modes, in a multiplicity of combinations and variations, is a sign of present health and provides a flexibility that bodes well for the future of American drama.

It took some time for our American playwrights to come to terms with the shocking, chaotic conditions of the 1960s and to incorporate into their thinking and writing the vision and techniques offered by the European Absurdist writers. It is for this reason that the mid-1960s was a relatively undistinguished period of American drama. But behind the scenes the theatre was in ferment and, by the end of the decade, American dramatists finally integrated the Absurdist mode into their writing, discovering that it offered an effective ethos for responding to the times. American drama is no longer the offspring of Ibsenite realism alone, or of the various experimental impulses that fed into it prior to the end of the 1960s. Rather, it is the child of a hybrid tradition: Ibsenite realism and European Absurdism. With the Ibsenite careful construction and vivid naturalistic detail and the Absurdist genre flexibility, imagistic power, psychological depth, and intellectual seriousness, the child is well endowed to grow, develop, and produce meaningfully in the future. As the works of Bullins, Guare, Rabe, Anderson, and Albee indicate, American drama was in an exciting and fertile period in the 1970s, and such significant accomplishments by American playwrights are an alluring promise of unprecedented dramatic achievement during the decades to come.

Notes

[1]Gerald Weales, "The Stage," *Commonweal*, 96, 10 March 1972, p. 15.

[2]Mark Goldman and Isadore Traschen, "Introduction to Modern Drama," *The Drama: Traditional and Modern* (Boston: Allyn and Bacon, 1968), p. 309.

[3]Mel Gussow, "Recalling Evolution of 'Seascape' Play, Albee Sees Tale Not of Lizard, but of Life," *The New York Times*, 21 January 1975, p. 40.

[4]Martin Esslin, *The Theatre of the Absurd* (New York: Doubleday, 1961), pp. 225-227.

[5]Bernard F. Dukore, "Off Broadway and the New Realism," *Modern American Drama: Essays in Criticism*, ed. William E. Taylor (Leland, Florida: Everett Edwards, 1968), p. 158.

[6]Dukore, p. 166.

[7]*Ibid.*

[8]*Ibid.*, p. 164.

[9]David Rabe, *Sticks and Bones* (New York: Viking Press, 1973), p. 233.

[10]Charles Marowitz, "Introduction," *Off-Broadway Plays*, vol. 2 (London: Penguin, 1972), p. 9.

[11]Henry Hewes, "The Playwright as Voyager," *Saturday Review*, 20 November 1973, p. 48.

[12]Esslin, p. 225.

Bibliography

Adler, Thomas P. "Theatre in Review." *Educational Theatre Journal*, December 1974, pp. 529, 530.

"Albee: 'I Write to Unclutter My Mind.' " *The New York Times*, 26 January 1975, II, p. 1.

Albee, Edward. *Seascape*. New York: Atheneum, 1975.

Anderson, Robert. *Solitaire/Double Solitaire*. New York: Random House, 1971.

Artaud, Antonin. Preface to *The Theater and Its Double*. Translated by Mary Caroline Richards. New York: Grove, 1958.

Barnes, Clive. "Albee's *Seascape* Is a Major Event." *The New York Times*, 27 January 1975, p. 20.

——. "Stage: Long Wharf Takes Wry Looks at Marriage." *The New York Times*, 2 March 1971, p. 29.

——. "Theater." *The New York Times*, 5 May 1975, p. 40.

——. "Theater: A Most Gifted Playwright." *The New York Times*, 8 November 1971, p. 53.

——. "Theater: Anderson's *Solitaire/Double Solitaire*." *The New York Times*, 1 October 1971, p. 33.

——. "Theater: John Guare's *House of Blue Leaves* Opens." *The New York Times*, 11 February 1971, p. 54.

Beaufort, John. "Can Stage Buck TV Success?" *The Christian Science Monitor*, 3 March 1973, p. 123.

——. "Controversial Drama Will Air Tomorrow After Being Vetoed." *The Christian Science Monitor*, 16 August 1973, p. 16.

161

———. "Television Pressures: From 50's to 70's." *The Christian Science Monitor*, 24 March 1973, p. 24.

Berkvist, Robert. " 'If You Kill Somebody.' " *The New York Times*, 12 December 1971, II, p. 3.

Bosworth, Patricia. "Yes for a Young Man's Fantasies." *The New York Times*, 7 March 1971, II, p. 1.

Brustein, Robert. "The Theater of Middle Seriousness: A Report on the Broadway Season." *Harper's*, March 1959, pp. 56–63.

———. *The Third Theatre*. New York: Simon and Schuster, 1958.

———. "Why American Plays Are Not Literature." *Harper's*, October 1959, pp. 167–172.

Bullins, Ed. *The Taking of Miss Janie*. (Unpublished.)

"CBS Drops Viet Drama." *The Christian Science Monitor,* 8 March 1973, p. 10.

Clurman, Harold. "Theatre." *The Nation*, 1 March 1971, pp. 285–286.

———. "Theatre." *The Nation*, 18 October 1971, p. 380.

———. "Theatre." *The Nation*, 22 November 1971, p. 539.

———. "Theatre." *The Nation*, 15 March 1975, p. 314.

———. "Theatre." *The Nation*, 5 April 1975, p. 414.

Daudet, Alphonse. "The Last Class." *What Is the Short Story?* Edited by Eugene Current-Garcia and Walter R. Patrick. Chicago: Scott Foresman, 1961.

Donohue, John. "*Sticks and Bones* on TV." *America*, 1 September 1973, p. 120.

Downer, Alan. "The Future of American Theater." *The American Theater Today*. New York: Basic Books, 1967.

Dukore, Bernard F. "Off Broadway and the New Realism." *Modern American Drama: Essays in Criticism*. Edited by William E. Taylor. Leland, Florida: Everett Edwards, 1968.

Durrenmatt, Friedrich. "Problems of the Theatre." *Theatre in the Twentieth Century*. Edited by Robert W. Corrigan. New York: Grove, 1963.

Esslin, Martin. *The Theatre of the Absurd*. New York: Doubleday, 1961.

Feldman, Burton. "Anatomy of Black Humor." *Dissent*, March/April 1968, pp. 158-160.

Fergussen, Francis. *The Idea of a Theatre*. Princeton: Princeton University Press, 1949.

Gent, George. "Rabe Protests Pirated Version of *Sticks and Bones* in Moscow." *The New York Times*, 13 March 1973, p. 31.

Gill, Brendan. "Among the Dunes." *The New Yorker*, 3 February 1975, pp. 75-76.

———. "No Place Like Home." *The New Yorker*, 9 October 1971, pp. 95-96.

———. "Rabe." *The New Yorker*, 20 November 1971, pp. 48-49.

———. "Real Play, False Play, No Play." *The New Yorker*, 11 March 1972, p. 82.

Goldman, Mark, and Traschen, Isadore. "Introduction to Modern Drama." *The Drama: Traditional and Modern*. Boston: Allyn and Bacon, 1968.

Guare, John. *The House of Blue Leaves*. New York: Viking Press, 1972.

Gussow, Mel. "Recalling Evolution of *Seascape* Play, Albee Sees Tale Not of Lizard, but of Life." *The New York Times*, 21 January 1975, p. 40.

———. "2d David Rabe Play to Join *Pavlo Hummel* at *Public Theater*." *The New York Times*, 3 November 1971, p. 43.

———. "Stage: Bullins' *Taking of Miss Janie*." *The New York Times*, 18 March 1975, II, p. 4.

Hewes, Henry. "Albee Surfaces." *Saturday Review*, 8 March 1975, p. 40.

———. "A Husband's Undoing." *Saturday Review*, 16 October 1971, p. 35.

———. "Only Winter Is White." *Saturday Review*, 27 November 1971, pp. 70-71.

———. "The Playwright as Voyager." *Saturday Reveiw*, 20 November 1973, p. 48.

———. "Under the Rainbow." *Saturday Review*, 20 March 1971, p. 10.

Hughes, Catharine. "Albee's *Seascape*." *America*, 22 February 1975, pp. 136-137.

———. "An American Nightmare." *America*, 18 March 1972, pp. 294-295.

———. *"Solitaire/Double Solitaire."* *America*, 23 October 1971, p. 322.

———. "White on Black." *America*, 31 May 1975, p. 427.

Kalem, T. E. "Air-Conditioned Hell." *Time*, 22 November 1971, p. 93.

———. "Primordial Slime." *Time*, 10 February 1975, p. 57.

———. "Requiem for the '60's." *Time*, 19 May 1975, p. 80.

———. "Who Killed the Bluebird?" *Time*, 11 October 1971, p. 74.

Kauffmann, Stanley. "Now and Also Then." *The New Republic*, 7 June 1975, p. 20.

———. *"Seascape."* *The New Republic*, 22 February 1975, p. 22.

———. "Stanley Kauffmann on Theater." *The New Republic*, 26 May 1973, p. 22.

———. *"Sticks and Bones."* *The New Republic*, 4 December 1971, p. 22.

Kernan, Alvin. Introduction to *The Modern American Theater: A Collection of Critical Essays*. Englewood Cliffs, New Jersey: Prentice-Hall, 1967.

———. "Albee's Unwritten Part." *The New York Times*, 2 February 1975, II, p. 5.

Kerr, Walter. "A Blurred Picture of a Decade." *The New York Times*, 11 May 1975, II, p. 5.

———. "It's All True, But Is The Truth Enough?" *The New York Times*, 10 October 1971, II, p. 1.

———. "The Most Striking New American Play." *The New York Times*, 4 April 1971, II, p. 3.

———. "The Remaking of the American Theatre." Lecture given at Boston College, Newton, Massachusetts, 2 November 1976.

———. "Unmistakably a Writer—Why, Then, Does His Play Stand Still?" *The New York Times*, 14 November 1971, II, p. 3.

Kroll, Jack. "Leapin' Lizards." *Newsweek*, 10 February 1975, p. 75.

———. "Theater." *Newsweek*, 29 November 1971, p. 100.

———. "Theater." *Newsweek*, 20 December 1971, p. 53.

Krutch, Joseph Wood. *The Modern Temper: A Study and a Confession*. New York: Harcourt Brace, 1929.

Leone, Vivien. "Notes From an Accidentally Passionate Playgoer." *Drama and Theatre* 10 (1971–1972), pp. 134–136.

Little, Stuart W. *Off-Broadway: The Prophetic Theater*. New York: Coward, McCann and Geoghegan, 1972.

Mackay, Barbara. "Studies in Black and White." *Saturday Review*, 12 July 1975, p. 52.

MacLeish, Archibald. "Ars Poetica." *The Human Season*, pp. 141–142. Boston: Houghton Mifflin, 1972.

"Marginalia: Albee Cited for *Seascape*." *The New York Times*, 25 December 1975, p. 27.

Marowitz, Charles. Introduction to *Off-Broadway Plays*, vol. 2. London: Penguin, 1972.

McCarthy, Mary. "The American Realist Playwrights." *On the Contrary*. New York: Farrar, Strauss, and Cudahy, 1961.

Miller, Arthur. *Death of a Salesman*. New York: Viking, 1949.

Nethercot, Arthur A. "The Psychoanalyzing of Eugene O'Neill." *Modern Drama*, December 1960, pp. 242–256.

Novick, Julius. "Very Funny—Or a Long Sick Joke?" *The New York Times*, 21 February 1971, II, p. 9.

Oliver, Edith. "Fugue for Three Roommates." *The New Yorker*, 24 March 1975, pp. 62–63.

———. "Off Broadway." *The New Yorker*, 20 February 1971, p. 90.

O'Neill, Eugene. *Long Day's Journey into Night*. New Haven: Yale University Press, 1956.

———. *Strange Interlude*. In *The Plays of Eugene O'Neill*. New York: Random House, 1955.

Popkin, Henry. "How Did *Sticks and Bones* Fare in Moscow?" *The Christian Science Monitor*, 26 May 1973, p. 14.

Rabe, David. "Each Night You Spit in My Face." *The New York Times*, 18 March 1973, II, p. 3.

——. *Sticks and Bones*. New York: Viking Press, 1973.

Rutenberg, Michael E. *Edward Albee: Playwright in Protest*. New York: Drama Book Specialist, 1969.

Simon, John. "Domestic Infernos." *New York*, 22 November 1971, p. 76.

Smith, Hendrick. "Soviet Sticks and Stones for David Rabe." *The New York Times*, 12 April 1973, p. 56.

Weales, Gerald. "The Stage." *Commonweal*, 10 March 1972, p. 15.

Williams, Tennessee. *The Glass Menagerie*. In *The Modern Theatre*. Edited by Robert W. Corrigan. New York: Macmillan, 1964.

Young, Charles M. "Is Rape a Symbol of Race Relations?" *The New York Times*, 18 May 1975, II, p. 5.

Index

DATE DUE

GAYLORD   PRINTED IN U.S.A.